WHAT IS THE BIBLE, REALLY?

And Why the Answer Really Matters

Jim Hoffine

Dare Publications
darepublications@gmail.com
Birmingham, AL

What Is the Bible, Really?
And Why the Answer Really Matters

Copyright © 2024 by Jim Hoffine

All rights reserved. Printed in the United States of America. No part of this book may be used or reproduced in any manner whatsoever without written permission except in the case of brief quotations embodied in critical articles and reviews. For permission write to darepublications@gmail.com.

To Brooke and Dalton,

Still the Two Greatest Joys and Lights of My Life

Acknowledgment

First of all, I'd like to thank Ms. Martha Williams, English language expert and teacher extraordinaire. She has checked all three of my books prior to publication and given selflessly of her time in so doing. I'd also like to thank an endless spectrum of teachers and academics who, over the decades, have contributed in many and diverse ways to my understanding of issues related to the Bible and its genesis. I am forever indebted to you all.

Table of Contents

Acknowledgment 5
Introduction 9
Chapter One: Which Bible? 12
Chapter Two: Why Does It Matter? 15
Chapter Three: The Influence of the Bible Throughout History 18
Chapter Four: A Very Brief History of How the Bible Was Birthed from Israelite Culture and The Early Church 21
Chapter Five: How the Individual Books Came to be Included in the Bible 28
Chapter Six: The Transmission of the Bible Books 32
Chapter Seven: Bible Translations 39
Chapter Eight: Problems within the Bible Itself (Hebrew Bible/Old Testament) 45
Chapter Nine: Problems Within the Bible Itself (New Testament) 51
Chapter Ten: Problems Between the Bible and Science 58
Chapter Eleven: The Bible's Influence on Individual Believers 64
Chapter Twelve: What is the Bible, Really? 70
Chapter Thirteen: What Should We Do with the Bible? 79
Chapter Fourteen: Final Thoughts 84

Introduction

The question posed on the cover of this book requires consideration of a *huge* amount of information; and, if one were to answer it in meticulous detail, we'd all be here until not one of us even cared what the answer is any more. And nobody has time for that.

But I believe the question of "What is the Bible, Really?" can be adequately answered with a whole lot fewer words, so don't despair. I will get right to the heart of the issues involved, and you'll have plenty of time to live your best life without getting sidelined by a boatload of details that only the extremely nerdy (or the overly obsessive) can stomach.

We'll begin with consideration of what we mean when we say, "The Bible." Your first response to that statement may well be, "What are you talking about? *Everyone* knows what the Bible is!" And to some degree, you'd be right. But if you were to ask a devout Jewish person, a devout Catholic person, a devout Protestant person, or a devout Eastern Orthodox person that question, you're likely to get four different answers. So it's necessary to define our terms as we get started.

From there we'll look into all kinds of related matters, like "Is it a book, or a collection of books?" "Who wrote it?" "Who decided which books should be included in THE book?" "How did it get copied through the centuries, since there was no such thing as a printing press until about a millennium and a half after the last individual book was written?" "What languages were used to write the books?" And, of course, we'll consider the question of "Why should anyone care?"

This last question has sort of a simple answer, because, if The Bible is what some say it is—a written communication from an eternal God to mankind that reveals a universe of reality not physically seen or heard by anyone living today—then its importance would dwarf the importance of any other book ever written on this planet or another.

If, on the other hand, it is *not* a communication from an unseen God, then its importance would not necessarily be more or less than any other book you might find in your local bookstore.

In case you're wondering what my qualifications are for writing this book, I will simply say that, for over fifty years, I've considered the fundamental question of what the Bible actually is. And in the process, I've studied the original languages used to write it, the historical, geographical, and religious backgrounds of the people who wrote it, the groups who collected the individual books and declared them to be "holy," and related literatures and topics. Specifically, I earned a Bachelor's and a Master's degree in Bible and Biblical Languages at an evangelical Bible College, then a Master's and a Ph.D. (ABD) degree in Hebrew language and Hebrew Bible at the University of Wisconsin (Madison main campus). And since then I've taken a number of Bible-related courses online from various universities, and of course nearly read myself blind in books both near and far to the general topic.

As you can probably tell from that summary, I *love* the study of all things Bible and Bible-related, and of the many cultures and histories that gave rise to that "book." And it is my purpose here to introduce the reader to some information that he, she, or they may not be familiar with—with the ultimate goal of providing a substructure of knowledge the reader can use to form their own opinion about what The Bible is.

It's an interesting study, at the very least, and having *more* information rather than *less* is always a good thing. So let's get right into it, and hopefully some questions you may have had over your lifetime about the Bible and its origin will be answered. If you have any additional questions after reading this book, or need clarification about any of the information covered here, you can always email me at jimhoffine@aol.com. My digital door is always open, and I'm more than happy to respond to the best of my ability.

Please note: In referring to dates, I will use the modern appellations of BCE (Before the Common Era) and CE (Common Era) instead of the earlier BC (Before Christ) and AD (Anno Domini—"Year of Our Lord"). They indicate the same exact divisions of time, but are less religious in nature. Most quotes from the Bible will come from the NRSV (New Revised Standard Version), which in my opinion is the best modern English translation on the market. It is free of theological influence, and is quite faithful to the original Bible languages.

Jim Hoffine
Birmingham, AL
2024

Chapter One

Which Bible?

If you were to walk down any random street in almost any country, and ask the passers-by, "What is The Bible?," you would get a variety of responses. I don't suggest that you do this on *any* street in *any* town anywhere, because you're likely to get looks of "Who is this cuckoo bird?" as a result. But here's the point. A devoutly Jewish person will say, "Why, The Bible means the 'Tanach,' what Christians call the Old Testament." A devoutly Protestant Christian will likely say, "Why, it's the Old and New Testaments, comprised of 66 books." A devoutly Catholic person will no doubt respond, "Why, it's the Old Testament, The Deuterocanonical Books, and the New Testament —73 books." And an Eastern Orthodox Christian would likely say, "Why, it's The Old and New Testament, plus other sacred writings—81 books!"

And if you single out certain individuals or groups within the overall Jewish or Christian traditions, you'll get even more disagreement. For example, the Samaritans, who trace their lineage back to ancient Israel in the First Millennium BCE (BC), claim that only the first five books of the Old Testament (Hebrew Bible) are sacred and of divine origin. (There are only about 1000 Samaritans left in Israel today, and they occupy a space in the northern West Bank area). And if you had asked Martin Luther—acknowledged as the founder of Protestant Christianity—he would've said that four of the commonly accepted New Testament books (Hebrews, James, Jude, and the Book of Revelation) don't belong in the

Bible. He called the book of James "an epistle of straw," meaning that he thought it was worthless (and therefore not of divine origin).

But none of this matters for the purpose of this book's argument. If it's called "The Bible"—whether composed of 5, 39, 66, 73, or 81 individual books, or some combination thereof—then it qualifies for our discussion.

One other issue should be mentioned here, which is that the names and order of books differs between Jews and Christians in the Old Testament (Hebrew Bible). For example, the first book of the Bible is called "Genesis" by Christians, but "Bereshith" ("In the beginning," Heb. בראשית, the first words of the book) by Jews. Also, the order of books in the Old Testament (Hebrew Bible) is different. For example, the Jewish canon treats the twelve shorter "books of the prophets" as one book, named "The Book of the Twelve." Christians, however, treat each prophetical book, whether short or long, as independent on its own. Thus, the Hebrew Bible contains 24 books, while the Christian Old Testament contains 39. It's the same exact material, but organized differently. Interestingly, since all the prophets are arranged together as a unit by the Jewish canon ("The Prophets," Heb. הנביאים), the last book of the Hebrew Bible (Old Testament) is 2nd Chronicles, while the last book of the Old Testament (Hebrew Bible) in the Protestant Christian canon is Malachi.

But again, none of this matters for the purposes of our discussion. If it's called "the Bible" by any group—Jewish, Christian, or otherwise—then it is the focus of this discussion.

The following chart will give you an idea of the disagreements which exist among the various religious communities in answering the question, "What is the Bible?," There is plenty of overlap among these lists, but there is plenty of uniqueness to each as well.

Jewish and Christian Bibles: A Comparative Chart

HEBREW BIBLE (a.k.a. TaNaK/Tanakh or Mikra)	Orthodox Christian OT (based on longer LXX; various editions)	Catholic Christian OT (Alexandrian LXX, with 7 deutero-can. bks)	Protestant Christian OT (Cath. order, but 7 Apocrypha removed)
Torah / Books of Moses 1) *Bereshit* / Genesis 2) *Shemot* / Exodus 3) *VaYikra* / Leviticus 4) *BaMidbar* / Numbers 5) *Devarim* / Deuteronomy	**Pentateuch** 1) Genesis 2) Exodus 3) Leviticus 4) Numbers 5) Deuteronomy	**Pentateuch (Law)** 1) Genesis 2) Exodus 3) Leviticus 4) Numbers 5) Deuteronomy	**Law (Pentateuch)** 1) Genesis 2) Exodus 3) Leviticus 4) Numbers 5) Deuteronomy

Nevi'im / Former Prophets
6) Joshua
7) Judges
8) Samuel (1&2)
9) Kings (1&2)
 	
Nevi'im / Latter Prophets
10) Isaiah
11) Jeremiah
12) Ezekiel
13) The Book of the Twelve:
  Hosea, Joel,
  Amos, Obadiah,
  Jonah, Micah,
  Nahum, Habakkuk,
  Zephaniah, Haggai,
  Zechariah, Malachi
	Historical Books
	6) Joshua
	7) Judges
	8) Ruth
	9) 1 Kingdoms (= 1 Sam)
	10) 2 Kingdoms (= 2 Sam)
	11) 3 Kingdoms (= 1 Kings)
	12) 4 Kingdoms (= 2 Kings)
	13) 1 Chronicles
	14) 2 Chronicles
	15) 1 Esdras
	16) 2 Esdras (= Ezra + Nehemiah)
	17) Esther (longer version)
	18) JUDITH
	19) TOBIT
	20) 1 MACCABEES
	21) 2 MACCABEES
	22) 3 Maccabees
	23) 4 Maccabees
		Historical Books
		6) Joshua
		7) Judges
		8) Ruth
		9) 1 Samuel
		10) 2 Samuel
		11) 1 Kings
		12) 2 Kings
		13) 1 Chronicles
		14) 2 Chronicles
		
		15) Ezra
		16) Nehemiah
		17) TOBIT
		18) JUDITH
		19) Esther (longer version)
		20) 1 MACCABEES
		21) 2 MACCABEES
			Historical Books
			6) Joshua
			7) Judges
			8) Ruth
			9) 1 Samuel
			10) 2 Samuel
			11) 1 Kings
			12) 2 Kings
			13) 1 Chronicles
			14) 2 Chronicles
			
			15) Ezra
			16) Nehemiah
			
			17) Esther (shorter version)

Khetuvim / Writings 14) Psalms (150) 15) Proverbs 16) Job 17) Song of Solomon 18) Ruth 19) Lamentations 20) Ecclesiastes 21) Esther (shorter version) 22) Daniel (12 chapters) 23) Ezra-Nehemiah 24) Chronicles (1&2)	**Poetic Books** 24) Psalms (151) 25) Odes (w/ Prayer of Manasseh) 26) Proverbs 27) Ecclesiastes 28) Song of Solomon 29) Job 30) WISDOM of Solomon 31) SIRACH, a.k.a. Ecclesiasticus 32) Psalms of Solomon	**Wisdom Books** 22) Job 23) Psalms (150) 24) Proverbs 25) Ecclesiastes 26) Song of Solomon 27) WISDOM of Solomon 28) SIRACH, a.k.a. Ecclesiasticus	**Wisdom Books** 18) Job 19) Psalms (150) 20) Proverbs 21) Ecclesiastes 22) Song of Solomon
	Prophets 33) Hosea 34) Amos 35) Micah 36) Joel 37) Obadiah 38) Jonah 39) Nahum 40) Habakkuk 41) Zephaniah 42) Haggai 43) Zechariah 44) Malachi 45) Isaiah 46) Jeremiah 47) BARUCH 48) Lamentations 49) LETTER of JEREMIAH 50) Ezekiel 51) Daniel (2 extra chapters separate): 52) SUSANNA 53) BEL and the DRAGON	**Prophets** 29) Isaiah 30) Jeremiah 31) Lamentations 32) BARUCH (w/ LETTER of JER.) 33) Ezekiel 34) Daniel (14 chapters) 35) Hosea 36) Joel 37) Amos 38) Obadiah 39) Jonah 40) Micah 41) Nahum 42) Habakkuk 43) Zephaniah 44) Haggai 45) Zechariah 46) Malachi	**Prophets** 23) Isaiah 24) Jeremiah 25) Lamentations 26) Ezekiel 27) Daniel (12 chapters) 28) Hosea 29) Joel 30) Amos 31) Obadiah 32) Jonah 33) Micah 34) Nahum 35) Habakkuk 36) Zephaniah 37) Haggai 38) Zechariah 39) Malachi

compiled by Fr. Felix Just, S.J.   http://catholic-resources.org/Bible/

Now that we have that out of the way, let's have a look at the issue contained in the subtitle of this book: "Why does it matter?"

Chapter Two

Why Does It Matter?

It matters, primarily, because if the claim by Bible believers that this collection of books called The Bible is the "word of God," then no other literature compares in importance. Yes, if this Bible is the verbal communication from the living God to mankind, pulling back the curtain on another supernatural world that humans don't see, then I'd say that NOTHING compares in importance. Yes, if God has spoken to man in a book, answering his questions about the origin of life and the physical world, the nature of God, what happens when we die, what is expected of we mere mortals during our earthly sojourn, and what is going to happen in the future, then *what could be more important?* The answer, I think, is *nothing.*

If, on the other hand, the Bible is no more than a collection of books which express the ideas of a pre-scientific culture long past, then its importance is greatly diminished. One might consider it to be of importance for a number of reasons—much like we consider the writings of Homer, Plato, Shakespeare, and endless ancient writers to be important. Such books firmly place us into the time of those authors, revealing their thoughts and passions, their take on history, their musings about morality and the divine, and so forth. But no one that I am aware of considers those writings to be messages from a divine being. And no churches, synagogues, or mosques have been erected for people to congregate in and read these books as Holy Scripture.

Therefore, the choice about The Bible's nature is binary—it either *is*, or *is not*, a message from a divine being. There is no middle ground here, although there are a number of theologians and biblical academics that would at least partially disagree with me on that issue. For example, most Catholics regard the Bible as "the word of God"— but only as it is interpreted by the church. And neo-orthodox theologians assert that, while the dead letters of the Bible books are not necessarily God's words, they can *become so* when read with the right spiritual experience. And this is what I want to consider in the remaining pages of this book.

The way we answer this question about the Bible's nature has colossal implications. If it truly is a message from the unseen God, then I would suggest that every human being on this planet who can read should read every last word of it, and keep reading it to gain as full an understanding as they can. God is talking to you! and can there be anything more important than that? I am a little concerned that those who do believe the Bible is the word of God don't actually read much of it. They read certain "verses" here and there, and maybe now and again read a whole book of it from beginning to end, but few have read it in its entirety. I mean, we ponder over UFO (UAP) sightings and what they might mean for our place in the universe. We dig madly in the dirt to try and find ancient texts long lost, and when we find them we treat them as if they were newly discovered Holy Writ. But the Bible, translated into nearly every language on the planet, and easily attainable for most industrialized and educated societies, is perhaps the most acquired and least read book in the world.

However, if the Bible is *not* a communication from the Divine Being, then the implications are quite different. I suggest that if this were true, we ought not allow it an authoritative place in our lives and our society. We should treat it just like we do other ancient writings—immensely interesting, but possessing no insight into things not seen. And while one can read the book of Proverbs, for example, and gain some wisdom about common human experiences, this is no different than reading Marcus

Aurelius' *Meditations* and gaining some helpful hints about how to navigate life.

And those are the questions I want to answer in this book: "Is it, or is it not, a 'message from Heaven?' And what significance should we attach to it based on how we answer that question?"

But before we do that, I want to have a brief look at just how influential this Bible book has been throughout history, and in our modern age.

Chapter Three

The Influence of the Bible Throughout History

The influence of the Bible on global history is an immense and complicated topic, and if I were to give a detailed account of it we'd both be here until the "cows come home." (Whatever that means). And "ain't nobody got time for that."

But a quick summary of some of the major ways this book has influenced culture—especially Western culture—will be helpful in understanding just how deeply and forcefully it has done so.

If we take the "first" Bible, namely the Hebrew Bible (Old Testament) into consideration, we can say that it influenced the religious ideas and customs practiced in ancient Israel. The Hebrews are first noticed historically somewhere in the 12th Century BCE (BC), and their traditions about their origins began to be transmitted orally among their various tribes. These traditions included claims about their genealogical heritage, their god Yahweh, and their overall history. But it wasn't until about 500 years later that these traditions began to be written down by the religious authorities of the day, and the mass of the Hebrew Bible wasn't written (in its final form) until sometime during the 6th Century BCE (BC).

And given that there were many different "Judaisms" being practiced in early Israelite history, it's difficult to know just how influential this corpus of books was. Almost no ancient Hebrew could read or write to any great extent, so they were dependent upon the religious authorities who possessed these scrolls to tell them about their contents. At any rate, the traditions behind these books were alive and well and floating all over the land of Israel for many centuries, and the core ideas contained in them were no doubt the basis on which many Hebrews formed their national identity and perceived their religious responsibilities.

However, when Jesus of Nazareth came along around 6 BCE (BC), and there arose an "offshoot" of Judaism that became Christianity, new books were added to the Hebrew Bible (Old Testament) to reflect the new ideas. These books, circulated among these new "Christians," became known as "The New Testament," and by the 4th Century CE (AD) the "official" list of New Testament books was declared. This list has not changed from that time until the present, and it contains lots of different types of literature (gospels, letters, histories, apocalyptic predictions of the future). This new "testament" formed the basis of various types of Christianity, although the process of interpreting them is an ongoing phenomenon that shows no signs of letting up.

But the wide distribution of the Bible didn't happen until the invention of the printing press by Johannes Gutenberg about 1440 CE (AD) because, prior to that time, transmission of literature had to be done by hand—i.e., very slowly. But even so, the *very* wide distribution of the Bible didn't happen for many years afterward, because printing was an expensive process, and not everybody had the funds to be buying a Bible.

Today, of course, the distribution of the Bible is massive, and almost anyone who would like a copy can get one—often for free. (Many churches provide them at no cost, all libraries have them, hotel rooms have tiny New Testaments in their bedside drawers, and you can get the whole thing online if you have a computer and internet access).

In fact, *The Guinness Book of World Records* suggests that about 5-7 *billion* Bibles have been sold, making it THE best-selling book of all time. In short, there is hardly a home in the industrialized Western world that you can enter that does not have at least one copy of it sitting around somewhere.

But the crux of the matter is how it has influenced human behavior. Most Christians and Jews regard it as THE source book for answering the many questions they have about their lives and existence, although many Jews rely on their rabbis for guidance in helping them understand what it means and many Christians rely on their pastors or priests to do the same. And there is considerable conflict among these faith traditions about what should be the "correct" understanding of these texts. (E.g., Orthodox Jews are more "literal" in their treatment of their Bible, while Reformed Jews are more liberal about it. And the same goes for Christians, whether Protestant, Catholic, or Eastern Orthodox. There are both more "conservative" and more "liberal" communities and denominations among all these groups).

And while the Bible has provided a great deal of comfort and motivation for good to millions in the world, it has also spurred a lot of evil. For example, it was used to justify slavery in America in the 19th and early 20th Centuries, to cause harm (both socially and by violent physical acts) against LGBTQ+ folks, and to justify xenophobia (the fear and hatred of others who don't look or speak like you). And just think about the Crusades and the Spanish Inquisition, when the Bible and its associated religion were used in the service of warfare and torture. It's been a mixed bag in terms of its influence, but no one can deny its oversized influence on cultures around the world.

So how did the individual books of the Bible get written down and transmitted all over the world? That will be the focus of our next few chapters, and we'll look at the history of Israel and the early Church which was the social and geographical birthplaces of these writings, the actual writing process (before there was such a thing as a printing press), and related issues. It's a fascinating study, and well worth your time.

Chapter Four

A Very Brief History of How the Bible Was Birthed from Israelite Culture and The Early Church

It is important to know a little about the history of the Hebrew people (later known as "Israelites," and then "Jews") because it is that culture which gave rise to what is known as The Hebrew Bible (Old Testament). Stories, laws, histories, poetry, wisdom sayings, prophecies, and liturgies arise out of specific cultures, and almost all cultures have them. Arab/Muslim culture gave rise to the Koran, Hindu culture birthed The Vedas, Japanese culture produced the Shinto books called "The Analects," and so forth.

And so it was with the Hebrews. These books in the Hebrew Bible did not suddenly appear from Heaven, written on holy scrolls, and then float to earth. They contain the oral and written traditions developed by a people who occupied Palestine (roughly modern Israel) from about 1200 BCE (BC) to around 70 CE (AD)—but not continuously. Their volatile history accounts for a fair amount of the Bible's literature, because every couple of hundred years they were either fighting amongst themselves, or powerful foreign nations were subduing them or carrying them off into captivity. That kind of trouble weighs on a people's spirit, and elicits questions like, "Why is this happening to us all the time?"

So what, in a nutshell (and a very small one), is the story of Israel's history?

If you use The Hebrew Bible (Old Testament) as the source for that history, then the picture is pretty simple. A man named Abram (later, "Abraham") from the city of Ur in Mesopotamia (modern day dig site Tell el-Muqayyar in southern Iraq) was told by the Hebrew god Yahweh to go to Canaan (modern day Israel) somewhere around 2000-1700 BCE (BC). He did so, and fathered Isaac, who later fathered Jacob. This last son was renamed "Israel," and he fathered twelve sons whose descendants became the twelve tribes of Israel.

After militarily subduing the native Canaanites, these twelve tribes settled most of what is modern day Israel, and they were governed by tribal leaders known as "judges." However, the people wanted a king (like the other nations around them), so somewhere around 1000 BCE (BC) Saul was "anointed" as the first one. He was followed by his son Jonathan's close companion, David, who was then followed by his son Solomon, and for a couple hundred years these early Hebrews existed as one unified nation. However, squabbling arose among them (as is often the case with human beings), and the *unified* nation split into *two* nations—*Israel* in the north, and *Judah* in the South. (The nation of Judah was named after the eldest son of Jacob, who served as one of the dominant tribal heads of the sons of Jacob).

But around 721 BCE the Assyrians from the northeast came and carried off most of the two northern tribes ("Israel"), and around 586 BCE the Babylonians from the northeast came and carried off the elite portions of Judah, as well as a significant number of regular citizens. Then, the Persians/Medes defeated the Babylonians, and sent the captive Judah-ites back to Israel, where they rebuilt their temple that the Babylonians had destroyed. But around 323 BCE (BC) the Greeks, under Alexander, rolled through the entire Middle East and subdued everyone. And after this, the Romans defeated the Greeks (around 146 BCE), and at the time of Jesus (6 BCE-30 CE?), Israel (an interchangeable name for Judah at this time) was under strict Roman rule.

Pretty straightforward history, eh?

And one might be tempted to accept the Hebrew Bible as accurate history, except for the fact that it also contains such eye-popping events as snakes and donkeys talking, a global flood, an inferred claim that the earth is about 6-8 thousand years old, the abrupt stoppage of the sun's movement so a battle could continue, a young fellow swallowed and then regurgitated by a big fish, Moses' cutting a path through the Red Sea with a shepherd's staff, sticks turning into snakes, folks walking on water, and etc. etc. etc. Therefore, one might well question if any historical claim in the entire book is trustworthy.

The first mention of "Israel" from *outside* the Hebrew Bible is in an inscription from 1208 BCE (BC) found on "The Merneptah Stele." This is a *stele* (a tall stone or wooden slab with images and writing inscribed on it, often to memorialize a king or other dignitary) that is alleged to have been commissioned by Egyptian Pharoah Merneptah (1213-1203 BCE?) and it reads "Israel is laid waste, his seed is no more." (Though some modern scholars quibble with this translation). But there is no other known reference to Israel or the Hebrews by any outside nation at any time before this—which would be odd for the times, if they did in fact exist as a nation.

Merneptah Stele, 1205 BCE

So here is my take on what most likely is the truth of Israel's history:

Sometime around 1300 BCE, some sub-tribe of Canaanites (Semitic peoples living in Canaan (roughly the geographical area of modern Israel, who spoke languages closely related to Hebrew), established themselves as a separate people, and began to develop the traditions we find in the Bible. They began to subdue their fellow Canaanite tribes by force, and established governance under tribal leaders known as "judges." However, after a while they wanted to have a king, and a kingdom, like other powerful nations surrounding them, so they "elected" Saul to the post. This brings us to around 1000 BCE (BC), when Saul was replaced by Israel's most famous king, David. Over the next 200 years, David's son Solomon and his offspring ruled over a more or less united Israel, but as people are inclined to do over time, they fought amongst themselves, and ten of the original twelve "tribes" of Israel established a separate kingdom in the south of Canaan and took on the moniker, "Judah." (After Jacob's son Judah, and likely because it was the largest tribe with the most sophistication). I am not convinced that this series of events happened exactly like that, but it was probably similar to that.

Meanwhile, the powerful Assyrians to the East sauntered on over to the Northern Kingdom (Israel) and carried a large amount of its population into captivity in Assyria (about 721 BCE). Those two tribes, over time, then intermarried with these Assyrians, and thus the Northern Kingdom existed no more as a unique bloodline culture, and were never to return to their homeland.

Meanwhile, in the Southern Kingdom, "Judah," life was fairly stable, until the powerful Babylonians from the East came and destroyed the Jerusalem (First) Temple and carried off most of the upper echelon (leaders, scribes, artists, the wealthy, etc.) to Babylonia. You can hear the gloom and longing to go home felt by these folks in the verse of an exilic Psalm:

By the rivers of Babylon—
there we sat down, and there we wept
when we remembered Zion. (Psalm 137:1)

But this was not the end for the Jews (now called "Jews," or "Yehudiym" after the nation name "Judah"). The Persian King Cyrus, for probable pragmatic and economic reasons, decided to let those Jews remaining in Persia (now thus called after the Persians defeated the Babylonians for control of that land), go back to their homeland (around 538 BCE). They did so, rebuilt their Temple (known now as The Second Temple), and life was good—for a while.

But as geo-political power was changing fairly frequently in those days, the Greeks under Alexander (about 323 BCE) came rolling though that area of the world and everything changed. The culture in Judah, and in the areas surrounding it, became "Hellenized," and soon everyone was speaking Greek and adopting the religious and cultural practices of their conquerors. This, of course, is why the New Testament (beginning to be written around 50 CE (AD) is written in Greek and not in Hebrew (or its cousin Aramaic).

As for the origin of the New Testament itself, and the "church" which was being spawned simultaneously, one must look to the religious movement begun by Jesus of Nazareth (around 27 CE/AD?). This (almost certainly historical) character had a new way of defining religion and religious obligation. His teachings were collected, probably at first orally, and then written down in various "books" that began to circulate among those communities that had been "evangelized" by the early apostles.

Jesus' speeches, dialogues, travels, and life events are found mostly in the Four Gospels, but here again the "fantastic, extraordinary, and mind-boggling" events woven into these gospels might well cause a reasonable person to question just how much of the history of Jesus and the early church really happened that way. I mean, we have such supernatural events going on as demons being cast out of individuals and taking up residence in pigs who then drown themselves in a lake, dead people being "resurrected" (not just Jesus, but also Lazarus, the son of the widow from Nain, and the daughter of Jairus), the healing of folks with leprosy and the inability to walk by just a word or a touch, the acute reattaching of a Roman centurion's ear after Peter cut it off, the changing of common water into wine (nice!), the "family size" meal created from just a couple of loaves of bread and a few fishes ("family size" here meaning a family of 5000 people!), and etc. Pretty *in*credible stuff.

But the issue most important to note here is that Christianity was born out of Jesus' words and deeds, and then by his followers who took that narrative outside of Palestine and into the then-known world. At first, it was an offshoot of Judaism (the religion of the Jews), but then became "its own thing," and over the last 2000 years has morphed into something a bit different than its very primitive form. What passes for Christianity these days, especially among the hyper-conservative branch of Christian believers known as "evangelicals" or "fundamentalists," bears little resemblance to the teachings of Jesus recorded in the Gospels. It is more of a religio-political dogma, in which the pure essence of Jesus' teaching is distorted. But more on that later.

If you take nothing else from this chapter, I hope you'll at least see that the books of the Bible reflect responses to real troubles and questions that the Israelites, and later the Christians, were experiencing in their own times. The major prophets (Isaiah, Jeremiah, Ezekiel) were trying to explain to the Israelites why they were getting their butts kicked every now and again (it was their sin and the abandoning of their God), but these prophets also wanted to encourage them that in future times God would restore them to their land and a safe and prosperous existence.

In the case of the New Testament, all the books positioned after the Gospels deal with real troubles and challenges that the "Church" was having from within and without their communities, and how the New Testament writers proposed to resolve those issues, while the Gospels themselves purport to tell the story of the life and times of Jesus of Nazareth.

Next up, we'll have a look at just *how* the specific books that are included in the various Bibles came to be included in them.

Chapter Five

How the Individual Books Came to be Included in the Bible

So, did the separate Bible books appear on a big list of religious writings in ancient history, and then some council of religious leaders said "yes" to some and "no" to others?—you know, "these particular books are 'inspired' and these other books are not."

Not exactly.

The history of the *canonization* of certain Bible books is a complex and not fully understood subject, but here are the nuts and bolts of it. ("Canon," by the way, is a Greek term meaning "rule" or "approved list," first used in the 4th Century CE/AD by Christian leaders to refer to religious writings that were "inspired by God," and thus worthy of being included in their Bibles. If a book like The Gospel of Matthew was deemed to be "inspired," it was said to be "canonical." If a book like The Gospel of Thomas was not deemed to be inspired, it was said to be "non-canonical" and was not included).

As far as the Hebrew Bible (Old Testament) goes, it came out of the various "Judaisms" that were prevalent in the earliest days of the nation. Judaism was not "monolithic" (one single, unified religion with no variations in perspective) at that time, nor is it today, and this was evident even as late as Jesus' time (see His discussion with the woman at the well in John 4:4-42). In other words, there were lots of religious and historical writings circulating in those days (see, for example, the reference to "The Book of Jashar" in Josh. 10:12-13; 2 Sam. 1:17-27), and the religious authorities felt obliged to declare which books were to be regarded as holy and divine and authoritative. And while most of its "canon" had been decided upon by the time of Ezra in the 4th Cent BCE (BC), a few books (like Daniel and Chronicles) had not been written yet, and they were only later considered worthy of inclusion.

And Judaism in general arranged these 24 books into 3 sections: "The Law" ("Torah"), "The Prophets" (Nebiim"), and "The Writings" ("Ketubiim"). By the way, the first letters of those Hebrew words "**T**orah," "**N**ebiim," and "**K**etubiim" form the acronym "TNK," pronounced "Tanach," and "Tanach" is what modern Jews call their Bible these days. Of course, adding to the confusion is the fact that many other books were written by religious Jews from the period of Ezra until about 100 BCE (BC), and many of these were included in the most popular translation of the existing Hebrew Bible of the day—"The Septuagint" (known as "The LXX," or "The Seventy," thus called because there were allegedly 72 separate scholars who translated the Hebrew Bible into Greek without collaboration, and their translations matched WORD FOR WORD, thus proving that the LXX was a miraculous translation and thus "God-approved." Hint: This is an absurd claim, and it didn't happen. But since most Jews in those days had been Hellenized, and Greek was their primary language, this translation was revered as sacred, and even some New Testament authors quote from it instead of the Hebrew of the original books).

A brief word about the alleged "Council of Jamnia" is appropriate here. This council of Jewish religious leaders was proposed by a 19th Cent. CE (AD) German scholar to have taken place in the latter part of the 1st Cent. CE, and was for the purpose of "finalizing" the approved list of books to be included in the Hebrew Bible. These Jewish leaders supposedly convened the council in response to this new "Christian" movement which, in their view, was distorting and perverting true Judaism. (I.e., these new Christian "apostles" like Peter and Paul were converting people into a new kind of Judaism which claimed Jesus of Nazareth as the prophesized "messiah" of the Old Testament, and were telling them that many of the customs and beliefs of Judaism were no longer to be observed). But the existence of such a council has almost no documentary support, and today most scholars don't believe that it ever happened. And anyway, the basic Jewish canon (Bible) was almost certainly already circulating a few hundred years earlier, maybe even from the time of Ezra in the 5th and 4th Cents. BCE (BC).

As far as the New Testament is concerned, its formation was an evolving process. The initial phase was the oral traditions about Jesus that circulated among these new "believers." Then these traditions began to be written down, and were collected and circulated as "gospels." At the same time, the "apostles" (the original twelve contemporaries of Jesus, minus Judas) were evangelizing across Israel, and north and southward via Paul and company, establishing "churches" that they wrote letters ("epistles") to over the years. These letters were then collected, and eventually brought into a "canon." The criterion for including these books was that they had to have "apostolic authority" — meaning either written by an apostle himself or by someone with direct connection to that apostle. (For example, the Gospel of Mark gained acceptance into the canon because, even though Mark was not an apostle, he was allegedly the Apostle Peter's "amanuensis," or "mouthpiece").

As time passed after Jesus was gone, these new Christian believers sprang up all over the regions around Israel, churches were formed, and church "fathers" or leaders arose. And, as one can imagine with groups of all kinds, not all these churches, believers, leaders, etc. agreed upon which circulating collection of books was to be considered "the Bible." But political realities of the day finally settled which slightly differing "canons" were to be acknowledged as divine or final. The Roman Emperor Constantine 1 called in 325 CE (AD) for a wide council of Christian leaders (bishops, elders, etc.) to be convened in Nicea (now Iznik, Turkey), and while the main topic to be decided was whether Jesus was a created being or The Eternal God (as Athanasius and his movement denied), the 27 books essentially acknowledged as the New Testament today were never seriously challenged after that (except in rare Catholic or Orthodox Christian quarters, where Revelation, James, Hebrews, etc. were questioned by some).

The formation of the Hebrew Bible canon and the New Testament canon were extremely complex processes, and I have barely skimmed the surface of those processes here, but they do have a common kind of evolution. And that commonality has to do with the *process*: First, oral traditions about principal religious figures and their histories are created, then those oral traditions are written down into "books," then those "books" are collected into a corpus or "canon," then the prevailing religious authorities lock down what the "official" canon is. And as we saw in Chapter 1, the Jewish folk regard the 24 books—the "Tanach"— as their Bible (which equals, in content, the 39 books of Protestant Christians' Old Testament), Protestant Christians regard the 66 books as theirs (39 for the Old Testament, 27 for the New), Catholic Christians regard the 73 books as theirs (46 for the Old Testament, 27 for the New), and Orthodox Christians regard the 81 books as their Bible (the 46 of the Old Testament, the 27 of the New, and various other books unique to their community).

Whew!!!! That's a lot of centuries, peoples, squabbles, and differences of opinion and belief, right? The essential point to be understood here is that the formation of any of these Bibles was a uniquely *human* undertaking, and as history always teaches us, different communities will sincerely come to different conclusions when religion, politics, or philosophies are in question.

So, next up, we'll have a look at how these "books," once written, were transmitted from place to place before the much later invention of the printing press in 1440 CE (AD).

Chapter Six

The Transmission of the Bible Books

If you want to copy something these days and send it to someone else, you will likely use your computer or cell phone to do so. There are various ways this can be done, from "copy and paste" computer options to capturing a picture on your phone and texting it to someone. Easy peasy.

However, in the ancient world, if you wanted to copy a document and transmit it somewhere else, the process was much more difficult. First of all, you would've had to be literate—able to read and write—and this was mostly only the privilege of the more wealthy and socially sophisticated. Second, you would've had to have something to write on, something to write with, and some form of "ink"— also mostly the domain of the wealthy and sophisticated.

And when the documents of the Hebrew Bible (Old Testament) were being written down and collected into a canon (about 700-160 BCE/BC), this process of copying and transmitting was accomplished by "scribes." In Israel, scribes were educated Jews who performed not only the task of copying important documents, but also performed legal, religious, and political functions. In other words, they were very important to the functioning of Jewish society. But once the documents were written and regarded as authoritative, these scribes had to have something to copy them onto. In the case of the Hebrew Bible (Old Testament), these "blank sheets of paper" were actually either "parchment" (dried out and scraped animal skins, usually from sheep or cows) or "papyrus" (glued together leaves from the Egyptian papyrus plant). So most of the "original" documents and the subsequent copies of them were written on one or the other of these materials. And for the Hebrew Bible (Old Testament), these documents were written onto individual "leaves," these leaves were then sewn (or glued) together, and finally they were rolled up onto sticks so as to form a "scroll."

The first picture shows the "pages" of a scroll attached together, the second shows how those pages were wrapped around "sticks" to form a scroll.

The "pens" utilized in Hebrew Bible times were actually "reeds," made by cutting down and shaping either bamboo or other plant stalks so that they had a sharp point on one end. The "ink" used was a diluted black paint made from carbon particles and a semi-liquid, sticky, or gummy substance. The carbon particles could come from cooking fire soot or other ash that produced a fine black powder. To keep the particles from clumping together, the mixture was combined with water and tree gum, which also helped the ink adhere to the writing surface.

A reed pen

The historical process of "copying," however, is quite complex. It was not a case of one scribe taking a very long manuscript and copying it word for word, although that was usually the scribe's goal. However, human beings are flawed by nature, and this copying suffered different kinds of "mistakes" over time. Here are some of the common ones, referred to by some fancy names:

- *homoearchy* – skipping a line (or lines) in the original manuscript because a previous line was textually similar and you "picked up" in the wrong place.
- *haplography* – Copying a word or syllable twice when it appears only once in the original text.
- *harmonization* – making your copy agree in wording with some other similar section of text because it is more familiar to you.
- *misreading a letter* – the Hebrew letter "kaph" (כ) is nearly identical in appearance to the Hebrew letter "beth" (ב), and one could easily be mistaken for the other.
- *intentional changes* - changing a word or phrase because you don't like (or agree with) what you are reading.

There are other types of mistakes, but you get the idea. And you can imagine that a scribe, tired and suffering eye fatigue after copying thousands of words, might make these kinds of errors. It happened a lot, and it's understandable. And add to this the fact that neither the original Hebrew Bible or New Testament originals used punctuation or word separation (!), so you can see why there are somewhere between 250-500 THOUSAND variances in our existing manuscripts of the Bible.

As an example of the occasional difficulty of knowing how to separate the letters according to the original author's intention, consider this phrase in English:

GODISNOWHERE (no punctuation or word separation, as in the biblical manuscript copies and originals).

Should it be read as "God is nowhere," or "God is now here"? Two *pretty* different meanings, right?

None of this would be a problem except for the fact that we have NONE of the original documents of either the Old or New Testaments. NONE!!!! They simply didn't survive, and we are left with trying to reconstruct them based on a comparison of the surviving thousands of copied manuscripts.

Early Hebrew script, written without vowels. There are separation spaces between words, but this is likely an innovation that came several hundred years after the earliest Old Testament manuscripts were written.

ΙѠΑΝΟΥ Β

ΟΠΡΕϹΒΥΤΕΡΟϹΕΚΛΕ
ΚΤΗΚΥΡΙΑΚΑΙΤΟΙϹΤΕ
ΚΝΟΙϹΑΥΤΗϹΟΥϹΕΓѠ
ΑΓΑΠѠΕΝΑΛΗΘΕΙΑΚΑΙ
ΟΥΚΕΓѠΜΟΝΟϹΑΛΛΑ
ΚΑΙΠΑΝΤΕϹΟΙΕΓΝѠΚ
ΤΕϹΤΗΝΑΛΗΘΕΙΑΝΔΙΑ
ΤΗΝΑΛΗΘΕΙΑΝΤΗΝΜΕ
ΝΟΥϹΑΝΕΝΗΜΙΝΚΑΙ
ΜΕΘΗΜѠΝΕϹΤΑΙΕΙϹ
ΤΟΝΑΙѠΝΑΕϹΤΑΙΜΕ
ΘΗΜѠΝΧΑΡΙϹΕΛΕΟϹ
ΕΙΡΗΝΗΠΑΡΑΘΥΠΑΤΡϹ
ΚΑΙΠΑΡΑΙΥ ΧΥΤΟΥΥΙ
ΟΥΤΟΥΠΑΤΡΟϹΕΝΑΛΗ
ΘΕΙΑΚΑΙΑΓΑΠΗ ΕΧΑ
ΡΗΝΛΕΙΑΝΟΤΙΕΥΡΗΚΑ
ΕΚΤѠΝΤΕΚΝѠΝϹΟΥ
ΠΕΡΙΠΑΤΟΥΝΤΑϹΕΝΑ
ΛΗΘΕΙΑΚΑΘѠϹΕΝΤΟ
ΛΗΝΕΛΑΒΟΜΕΝΠΑΡΑ
ΠΑΤΡΟϹΚΑΙΝΥΝΕΡѠ
ΤѠϹΕΚΥΡΙΑΟΥΧѠϹΕ
ΤΟΛΗΝΓΡΑΦѠΝϹΟΙΚ
ΝΗΝΑΛΛΑΗΝΕΙΧΟΜΕ
ΑΠΑΡΧΗϹΙΝΑΑΓΑΠѠ
ΜΕΝΑΛΛΗΛΟΥϹΚΑΙΑΥ
ΤΗΕϹΤΙΝΑΓΑΠΗΙΝΑ
ΠΕΡΙΠΑΤѠΜΕΝΚΑΤΑ
ΤΑϹΕΝΤΟΛΑϹΑΥΤΟΥ
ΑΥΤΗΗΕΝΤΟΛΗΕϹΤΙ
ΚΑΘѠϹΗΚΟΥϹΑΤΕΑ
ΠΑΡΧΗϹΙΝΑΕΝΑΥΤΗ
ΠΕΡΙΠΑΤΗΤΕΟΤΙΠΟΛ
ΛΟΙΠΛΑΝΟΙΕΞΗΛΘΟΝ
ΕΙϹΤΟΝΚΟϹΜΟΝΟΙΜΗ
ΟΜΟΛΟΓΟΥΝΤΕϹΙΝΧΝ
ΕΡΧΟΜΕΝΟΝΕΝϹΑΡΚΙ
ΟΥΤΟϹΕϹΤΙΝΟΠΛΑΝ
ΚΑΙΟΑΝΤΙΧΡΕΙϹΤΟϹ
ΒΛΕΠΕΤΕΕΑΥΤΟΥϹΙ
ΝΑΜΗΑΠΟΛΕϹΗΤΕΑΗΡ

ΓΑϹΑΜΕΘΛΛΑΛΜΙϹΘ
ΠΛΗΡΗΑΠΟΛΑΒΗΤΕΠΑϹ
ΟΠΡΟΑΓѠΝΚΑΙΜΗΜΕ
ΝѠΝΕΝΤΗΔΙΔΑΧΗΤΟΥ
ΧΥΘΝΟΥΚΕΧΕΙΟΜΕΝѠ
ΕΝΤΗΔΙΔΑΧΗΟΥΤΟϹΚ
ΤΟΝΠΑΤΕΡΑΚΑΙΤΟΝΥ
ΙΟΝΕΧΕΙ ΕΙΤΙϹΕΡΧΕΤΑΙ
ΠΡΟϹΥΜΑϹΚΑΙΤΑΥΤΗ
ΤΗΝΤΗΝΔΙΔΑΧΗΝΟΥ
ΦΕΡΕΙΜΗΛΑΜΒΑΝΕΤΕ
ΑΥΤΟΝΕΙϹΟΙΚΙΑΝΚΑΙ
ΧΑΙΡΕΙΝΑΥΤѠΜΗΛΕΓΕ
ΤΕΟΛΕΓѠΝΓΑΡΑΥΤѠ
ΧΑΙΡΕΙΝ ΚΟΙΝѠΝΕΙΤΟΙϹ
ΕΡΓΟΙϹΑΥΤΟΥΤΟΙϹΠΟ
ΝΗΡΟΙϹ ΠΟΛΛΑΕΧѠΝ
ΥΜΙΝΓΡΑΦΕΙΝΟΥΚΕΒΟΥ
ΛΗΘΗΝΔΙΑΧΑΡΤΟΥΚΑΙ
ΜΕΛΑΝΟϹΑΛΛΑΕΛΠΙΖΩ
ΓΕΝΕϹΘΑΙΠΡΟϹΥΜΑϹ
ΚΑΙϹΤΟΜΑΠΡΟϹΤΟΜΑ
ΛΑΛΗϹΑΙ ΙΝΑΗΧΑΡΑΥ
ΜѠΝΠΕΠΛΗΡѠΜΕΝΗ
Η· ΑϹΠΑΖΕΤΑΙϹΕΤΑΤΕ
ΚΝΑΤΗϹΑΔΕΛΦΗϹϹΟΥ
ΤΗϹΕΚΛΕΚΤΗϹ

ΙѠΑΝΟΥ Β

Early Greek script from the Fourth Cent. CE (AD).
Note that there is no separation between words.

This process of trying to reconstruct the wording of the originals from flawed copies is the science of "textual criticism," and it is pretty sophisticated and effective. So, to be fair, what we have in our Bibles is likely fairly close to what the authors of the original books wrote, but how can we be sure if we don't have those original manuscripts? If, say, a very early copy of Paul's letter to the Galatians had ten wording differences from what he originally wrote, then the copies that followed would have honestly repeated those errors, and even later copies may have introduced more errors.

In answering the question of "Why don't we have any of the original Bible documents?" some teachers at the very conservative Bible college I attended argued that if we had them, we might "worship" them. *Wut?* If we had them, then Jews and Christians could say that these originals are the unadulterated, pure "Word of God." I doubt there would be any "worshipping" of the documents themselves.

The main point here is that what we have in our Bibles probably represents the essence of what the original authors/editors wrote, but "essence" is not the same thing as "exact representation of." And when you claim that "God specifically penned each and every word of the Bible," but have to concede that He didn't perfectly preserve those very words in their original documents, then "Houston, we have a problem."

Another problem to consider—for those who claim that God wrote the Bible as his perfect message to mankind—is that both the Hebrew Bible and the New Testament were written in times when most common folk were illiterate, or at best semi-literate. In other words, even if the various farmers and artisans spread across the nation of Israel had ever seen any of these documents, they likely would've looked at them and said, "It's all Greek (or Hebrew) to me!" Kind of odd, if a deity were intending to get a message to them.

Next up, we'll have a look at Bible *translations*. These are the result of translating the original Hebrew, Aramaic, and Greek documents into other languages, like English, French, Spanish, German, and the hundreds of other languages that exist in the world. And there are different types of translations, depending on what the intent of the translators was.

Chapter Seven

Bible Translations

The Bible is the most translated book in the world, probably because it is also the most widely distributed book in the world. And it's the most widely distributed book in the world because it is foundational to the largest conglomeration of religions, both Jewish and Christian.

"Translation," of course, means (in this context) the rendering into other languages of the books of the Bible which were originally written in Hebrew, Aramaic, and Greek. If you go to the bookstore and buy a Bible in English, this is because the Hebrew, the Aramaic, and the Greek words of the original Bible manuscripts have all been rendered into English. And as with any literature that was not written in a language that can be understood by those without knowledge of those original languages, translation enables one to read all kinds of the world's literature that they would not otherwise be able to read. For example, if I want to read Dostoyevsky's *The Brothers Karamazov* or Tolstoy's *Anna Karenina*, I'd best find an English translation of them, because my proficiency in the original Russian is virtually non-existent. Or if I want to read *Les Miserables* by Victor Hugo, I'm going to need an English translation of it, since my facility in French is also pretty terrible.

And "translation" of the Bible (converting it from the original languages to other languages) is different from "transmission" of the Bible (copying and distributing the original or copied documents, but still in those original languages). I only mention this because I occasionally see the two concepts confused or conflated with one another.

But the main point of this chapter is to look at the process of translating the Bible into English, and how some translations are actually *interpretations* rather than strict *translations*, and how some translations are infected by the translator's theological bias.

The main thing I can say about translations at this point is that "Boy, there sure are a lot of them!!!" And some are more popular than others. The most popular English translation of the Bible, historically, is the so-called "King James Version," that version which was translated and published in and around 1611 CE (AD). It is a work of art in terms of its fidelity to the original Bible languages and its artful and poetic use of English phrases in its renderings. However, there are at least a couple problems with it from today's perspective: The Hebrew/Aramaic and Greek texts upon which it was based are not as "pure" or "accurate" as those that modern scholarship has provided us today (for example, John 7:53-8:11, "The Woman Caught in Adultery," was not an original part of John's Gospel, even though it's a great story); and the English of King James' day is quite a bit different than modern English, leading to difficulty in understanding what the biblical author is saying. (For example, Psalm 23:1, "The Lord is my shepherd, I shall not *want*." The word "want" in Old English means "to lack essential needs," not "desire something" as it does today. That would be awkward if understood in terms of modern English: "The Lord is my shepherd, but I'm not going to want that to be so.")

The practice of Bible translation has been going on for over 2000 years. Almost as soon as its original documents surfaced, there were various ethnic communities translating them into their native languages. But I am not concerned with that here. I'm only concerned with the English translations that have become popular in the English-speaking world.

Some of the more popular ones are The King James Version (1611 CE/AD), The New King James Version (1982 CE), The New International Version (2011 CE, revised edition), The New Revised Standard

Version (2021 CE, updated edition), The New American Standard Version (2020 CE, revised version), and The Living Bible (1971 CE). In order of popularity (most versions sold), they place as follows:

1) New International Version (NIV)
2) King James Version (KJV)
3) English Standard Version (ESV)
4) New Living Translation (NLT)
5) Christian Standard Bible (CSB)
6) New King James Version (NKJV)
7) Reina-Valera (RV, in Spanish)
8) New International Reader's Version (NIRV)
9) New American Standard Bible (NASB)
10) New Revised Standard Version (NRSV)

As far as translating methodology (the principles by which translation is done), there are basically two types:

1) The *formal* method (also known as the literal method)
2) The *dynamic* method (also known as the functional equivalent method)

In the strict literal method, the original Hebrew/Aramaic/Greek words are translated into English in very literal fashion. However, since these texts are between 2000 and 3000 years old, they contain many alien words and figures of speech that are naturally hard for the modern English-speaker (or speaker of any modern language) to understand. English, for example, contains the idioms "kick the bucket" and "buy the farm"— neither of which refers to anyone kicking an actual bucket or buying an actual farm. They both mean "to die." And so it is in the languages of the Bible. In the Hebrew of Ruth 4:11 it is said that "Rachel and Leah....built up the house of Israel." Of course, these famed biblical women were not carpenters or architects, so they never built anybody's living quarters or place of residence. So here, "build up a house" means to provide offspring for their husband Jacob (Israel).And the Hebrew language itself has certain grammatical peculiarities (a lot of them, actually), as for example in Genesis 2:17, where God tells Adam if he eats from the tree of the knowledge of good and evil......"*dying you shall die.*" This repeating of the verb form (in gerund and regular verb tense forms) is often used to express emphasis. And here it means something like, "you shall *surely* die." "No doubt about it." "You're going to be a goner." "Kaputski for you."

So the dynamic method is often used in these instances to convey the meaning of a phrase that would otherwise seem strange or difficult to understand for the English reader.

But there are other methods of translation used to produce readable Bibles, perhaps the most common of which is the "paraphrase" method. The Living Bible is an example of such, and it goes to the extreme in trying to put biblical phrases into understandable English and custom. But in so doing, it engages more in "interpretation" than "translation." For example, in 1 Samuel 17:33, King Saul warns David not to fight Goliath, saying, "You are not able to go against this Philistine to fight with him, for you are just a boy, and he has been a warrior from his youth." However, the Living Bible puts it this way: "Don't be ridiculous...How can a kid like you fight with a man like him? You are only a boy, and he has been in the army since he was a boy!" This rendering captures the basic essence of what Saul was saying, but with words that don't appear in the Hebrew original. So, The Living Bible should be regarded more as a running commentary by its author (Ken Taylor) than an actual translation. And there are plenty of places in the Bible where the meaning is not clear from the original wording, so Mr. Taylor's translation is nothing more than his opinion about what any given passage means.

Another irritating (to me) tendency in some translations is the injection of theological doctrine into a word or phrase. For example, in Isa. 7:14, the prophet was talking to King Ahaz of Judah and declared, "Therefore the Lord Himself will give you a sign: Behold, a young woman will conceive and give birth to a son, and she will name Him Immanuel." The word "young woman" (Heb. *almah*, אלמה) simply means "young woman" without regard to whether she is a virgin or not. (There is another perfectly good word in Hebrew, *bethulah*, בתולה that means "virgin"). Isaiah was simply telling the King that a young woman of their time would become pregnant and bear a son, name him "Immanuel" (meaning "God is with us"), and before that son was of independent moral age (i.e., still very young), the Assyrians would come and destroy the King's enemy, Israel. Therefore Ahaz should not make a treaty with Assyria, because God was going to fix the king's "Israel problem." There is nothing miraculous about a young woman having a baby, but Ahaz was told to consider this particular baby as a sign from God that his northern enemy, Israel, would soon no longer be a problem for him. In fact, as Isaiah chapter 8 narrates, this young woman does have the baby and Assyria did come and destroy Israel.

However, the NASB (New American Standard Bible) translates this word "virgin," not "young woman" as is the case, because this verse is a foundational one for evangelical Christians who believe in the virgin birth of Jesus. (And they are following the Gospel of Matthew's author in using the LXX translation of "virgin" for "young woman." Matthew, of course, was notorious for citing Old Testament passages as "proof" that Jesus was Israel's expected Messiah).

So this is a case where a particular English translation editorial board allows their theological bias to distort the rendering of a very simple Hebrew word, "young woman," into "virgin."

Whenever I am reading a translation of a non-English book into English, I want to be sure I am reading a strict (though idiomatic) translation of the original author's words, without the translator's opinions of its meaning or his paraphrasing involved. When a translator injects his opinion or loose paraphrasing into their work, they are taking away my ability to form my own opinion of a passage *based on the actual words written.*

So, in my opinion—-based on my own translation of about one half of the Hebrew Bible and one-half of the Greek New Testament, plus my own reading of numerous English translations—there is one translation that is the most faithful to the original texts of the Bible, and that is the NRSVue (the *New Revised Standard Version*—updated edition). This translation does not engage in theological bias or loose-cannon paraphrasing. When there is an uncertain meaning of a Greek, Hebrew, or Aramaic word or phrase, they footnote the options of meaning. When there is uncertainty about what the wording of the original Bible text may have been, they give you the different manuscript options in a footnote. Of course, this is not to say that it is the only translation worthy of use, because there is much to be commended in other modern English versions. But again, in the field of English translation options, I think the NRSVue is currently the best.

In the next few chapters we'll consider some of the more eye-popping statements in the Bible itself—seeming contradictions within the Bible itself, and seeming contradictions between the Bible and science. Things are about to heat up, so hold on to your hats!

Chapter Eight

Problems within the Bible Itself (Hebrew Bible/Old Testament)

If you are an avid reader of the Bible, and you don't have significant memory problems, you will often run into a passage or verse that seems to say something contradictory to some other passage or verse you had read previously. Consider the following:

A - "Then Saul said to his armor-bearer, 'Draw your sword and thrust me through with it, so that these uncircumcised may not come and thrust me through and make sport of me.' But his armor-bearer was unwilling, for he was terrified. *So Saul took his own sword and fell on it. When his armor-bearer saw that Saul was dead,* he also fell on his sword and died with him." (1 Sam. 31:4-5)

"David went and took the bones of Saul and the bones of his son Jonathan from the people of Jabesh-gilead, who had stolen them from the public square of Beth-shan, where the Philistines had hung them up, on the day *the Philistines killed Saul on Gilboa.*" (2 Sam. 21:12)

"So Saul died for his unfaithfulness; he was unfaithful to the Lord in that he did not keep the command of the Lord; moreover, he had consulted a medium, seeking guidance, and did not seek guidance from the Lord. Therefore *the Lord put him to death* and turned the kingdom over to David son of Jesse." (2 Chr. 10:13-14)

Do you see the problem? In the passage in 1 Sam. 31:4-5, the text states that Saul fell on his own sword... and became "dead" (as one might expect). In the passage in 2 Sam. 21:12, it says that the Philistines killed Saul on Mt. Gilboa. However, in 2 Chr. 10:13-14, it says that The LORD put him to death.

Poor Saul, it seems that everybody was out to get him. But he either killed himself (suicide), the Philistines killed him, or the LORD killed him according to these passages. It can't be all three at once.

But those who hold that there can be no contradictions in the Bible do not accept the face value of these biblical statements. They engage in some sleight-of-hand in trying to harmonize them, reminiscent of one using a whittling knife to make a square peg fit into a round hole. (See, for example, *Answers in Genesis*, https://answersingenesis.org/contradictions-in-the-bible/how-did-king-saul-die/).

What likely is happening in these three passages is that there were slight differences in the various Hebrew traditions floating around about Saul's death, and the compilers of these traditions reproduced them as they heard or read them, not being concerned about the obvious conflicts between them.

B – "Again the anger of the Lord was kindled against Israel, and *he incited David against them*, saying, 'Go, count the people of Israel and Judah.'" (2 Sam. 24:1)

"*Satan* stood up against Israel and *incited David to count the people of Israel.*" (1 Chr. 21:1)

This problem is pretty easy to see. Was it "The Lord" who did the inciting, or was it "Satan?"

Again, those who pre-emptively allow for no contradictions in the Bible use a "fancy' way of harmonizing this problem. And it usually goes something like this: "Satan was the active agent who incited David, but the Lord permitted it." Alternatively, some say, "God was *using* Satan to incite David." Please. If you have to resort to such egregious harmonizing to support a pre-conceived notion about the Bible's credibility, I would suggest that you don't have a fair-minded common sense. And furthermore, since the traditions found in 2 Sam. 24:1 were written down and first circulated somewhere in the 6th century BCE (BC), that would mean that the Jews who read or heard those traditions were left in the dark about who incited David to perform this "evil" act until nearly 200 years later when the Chronicler wrote his books (around the middle/end of the 4th century BCE). So the more likely reason for the discrepancy is that the Chronicler, writing later based upon the text in Samuel, saw the theological problem with claiming that God had incited David to do something sinful, and he "fixed it."

C – "*David* put his hand in his bag, took out a stone, slung it, and struck the Philistine on his forehead; the stone sank into his forehead, and he fell face down on the ground. So David prevailed over the Philistine with a sling and a stone, striking down the Philistine and killing him; there was no sword in David's hand. Then David ran and stood over the Philistine; he grasped his sword, drew it out of its sheath, and killed him; then he cut off his head with it." (1 Sam. 17:49-51)

"Then there was another battle with the Philistines at Gob, and *Elhanan* son of Jaare-oregim the Bethlehemite killed Goliath the Gittite, the shaft of whose spear was like a weaver's beam." (2 Sam. 21:19)

"Again there was war with the Philistines, and Elhanan son of Jair killed Lahmi the brother of Goliath the Gittite, the shaft of whose spear was like a weaver's beam." (1 Chr. 20:5)

"Wut?" "Huh?"

In this very familiar story of David versus Goliath, we have one passage stating that David killed him, one stating that Elhanan did, and one saying that Elhanan killed Goliath's brother "Lahmi." And to make things even more confusing, Elhanan is called "the son of Jaare-oregim" in one passage, and "the son of Jair" in another. What the heck is going here?

The most likely explanation is that, again, you have earlier traditions citing an otherwise unknown fellow named "Elhanan" killing the mighty Philistine Goliath, a divergent tradition saying this same person killed Goliath's *brother*, and a final one in which this "heroic" legend was transferred to the mighty and heroic King David. The compilers of these Hebrew traditions seem not to be very concerned about apparent contradictions as they record the "sacred" sagas of Israel's heroes, and only concerned with writing them down as they find them.

So what do those who are zealous for biblical inerrancy and accuracy do with these passages? Why, what they do elsewhere, all the time. They say, "Well, the name Elhanan was actually King David's name before he was king," but they can provide no such evidence of that being so. Or they say, the name "Elhanan" was a scribal mistake, and the original text read "David," again with zero evidence that's the case (there is NO manuscript of the Hebrew Bible in existence with "David" as the name in these Elhanan passages). Or, even worse, they just say "That's one of the Bible's *great mysteries*, and one day we'll see the light." Great mysteries? I'd say there is no mystery at all here. We have contradictory versions of alleged historical events in the Bible that cannot be reconciled, even by the cleverest of arguments.

There are hundreds, if not thousands, of these kinds of contradictions in the Bible, and if I were to list and briefly discuss them all, that book would be significantly longer than Proust's *Remembrance of Things Past*, which totals about 3500 pages.

For your further consideration, have a look at *The Skeptic's Annotated Bible* which illuminates tons of them. In my opinion, they occasionally see a contradiction where there really isn't one (or at least it's not clear there is), but you'll get a feel for how large this issue is.

And let me mention one final thing about the Hebrew Bible (Old Testament). Most of it is written in the ancient Hebrew language, but there are significant portions of it written in its close cousin, Aramaic. But those who assert that the Bible is the written "Word of God" have no (credible) answer as to why this is the case. I mean, if God wants to speak to mankind, why in the world would he switch up languages midway through the process? And add to that the fact that the New Testament is written in Greek, and what we have (allegedly) is God using THREE different languages to communicate to mankind, most of whom have no understanding of, or facility in, *any* of these three. Kind of seems like he could've used some other form of communication that every human being (from day one) could understand. And if you consider that most people need to have these three languages translated into their own native tongues, and that sometimes the specific meaning of a word or phrase cannot be accurately translated into another language, then we start to get into the realm of the silly when claiming the Bible to be "God's Word."

And don't even get me started on the claim that God "wrote" or "inspired" his message in the original documents, but was unable (or unwilling) to maintain a perfect line of transmission of those documents. Yeah, right—he gave us his perfect word, but in the copying process he allowed it to be corrupted by ham-handed (or malevolent) copyists so that we only have "an approximation" of what his original documents said. I might have been born at night, but it wasn't *last* night!

Add to this the fact that ancient Hebrew writing did not have symbols for the vowels of the spoken language—vowels which are often critical in clarifying what specific "tense" or "mode" the consonants indicate, or how a noun is supposed to be pronounced and understood (which can leave the reader to guess about what actual word is indicated in a given phrase), then we're fully into the realm of the absurd. (Granted, in most places in the Hebrew Bible the meaning is made clear by the context, but there are hundreds in which it isn't).

And as one last morsel for your thought, why would a divine being feel compelled to communicate with his creatures by means of a "book" (or books), especially since in ancient times very few people could even read. (This changed, somewhat, by the time the New Testament documents were written, but not everyone in that world was literate, either). Why not appear to your creatures and speak in a language that EVERYONE could understand (supernaturally enabled by you, the Divinity), or even telepathically? Or maybe even write across the sky what you want your creatures to know, and make it permanently visible to all sides of the planet and for all time?

And since there are even questions about which books constitute the legitimate "Bible," and there is no unified understanding of what is written in them (check out the hundreds of different and contradictory interpretations by theologians from every faith community over the centuries), then a reasonable person might well conclude that either 1) God is not very effective at communicating with mankind, or 2) he didn't want to be clear in his communication, or 3) the whole idea of a deity communicating through "books" is an absurd notion on its face. (*Ding, ding, ding,* I choose what's behind door number three here).

Now, on to some "problems" in the New Testament.

Chapter Nine

Problems Within the Bible Itself (New Testament)

Here are just a few of the internal problems (contradictions) one can find in the New Testament:

A - After Peter bragged to Jesus that he would never deny Him, the author of Matthew's Gospel says Jesus responded this way:

"Truly I tell you, this very night, *before* the cock crows, you will deny me three times." (Matt. 26:34)

However, the author of Mark's Gospel has it a little differently:

"Truly I tell you, this day, this very night, before the cock crows *twice*, you will deny me three times." (Mark 14:30)

and….

"While Peter was below in the courtyard, one of the female servants of the high priest came by. When she saw Peter warming himself, she stared at him and said, 'You also were with Jesus, the man from Nazareth.' But he denied it, saying, 'I do not know or understand what you are talking about.' And he went out into the forecourt. *Then the cock crowed.* [And the female servant, on seeing him, began again to say to the bystanders, 'This man is one of them.' But again he denied it. Then after a little while the bystanders again said to Peter, 'Certainly you are one of them, for you are a Galilean, and you talk like one.' But he began to curse, and he swore an oath, 'I do not know this man you are talking about.' At that moment the cock crowed for the second time. Then Peter remembered that Jesus had said to him, 'Before the cock crows twice, you will deny me three times.' (Mark 14:66-72).

See the problem here?

Matthew's Gospel has Jesus telling Peter that he'll deny Him *three* times *before the cock crows*. Mark's Gospel, however, has Jesus wording it differently, saying, "Before the cock crows *twice*, you'll deny me three times." OK, so not a *big* problem, until Mark fleshes out the details in verses 66-72:

1) Peter denies Jesus.
2) The cock crows the first time.
3) Peter denies Jesus two more times.
4) The cock crows the second time.

In other words, Mark's recounting of events is in direct contradiction with what Jesus told Peter in Matthew—i.e., that b*efore* a cock would crow, Peter would have already denied Jesus three times.

Those who advocate for the Bible's perfection and inerrancy offer various explanations for the problem:

1) The word "second" does not appear in the original manuscript of Mark 14:30. This would remove the difference in what Jesus actually was to have said to Peter, but there is NO evidence (besides a couple of minor *very* late and unreliable manuscripts) that the original Mark manuscript had anything other than "a second time." And even if one accepted that ridiculous supposition, it still doesn't explain the detailed events given to us in Mark 14:66-72.

2) The "cock crowing the second time" in Mark's recounting of events is actually what is referred to in Matthew's "before the cock crows." In other words, Matthew's *single* crowing is actually Mark's *second* crowing. Sheesh, talk about trying to fit a square peg into a round hole!

B - And consider this problem between Mark's Gospel and that of Luke:
"Then Jesus gave a loud cry and breathed his last. And the curtain of the temple was torn in two, from top to bottom." (Mk. 15:37-38)

"It was now about noon, and darkness came over the whole land until three in the afternoon, while the sun's light failed, and the curtain of the temple was torn in two. *Then* Jesus, crying out with a loud voice, said, "Father, into your hands I commend my spirit." Having said this, he breathed his last." (Luke 23:44-46).

See the problem?

In Mark, Jesus dies, then the curtain in the Temple was torn in tow from top to bottom," (This curtain, by the way, was the one separating the outer Temple court from the "Holy of Holies," a section of the Temple where God was believed to have lived in some physical form—see Ex., chapters 25-31). In Luke, however, the order of events is reversed. While Jesus is still on the cross, *alive*, the Temple curtained is torn, and *then* Jesus dies.

Those who argue for a perfect Bible again use a little translational sleight-of-hand here. Their argument is that the Greek word (kai, και), often translated here as "then," doesn't necessarily imply chronological order. In other words, they're saying that the "tearing" and the "dying" occurred at exactly the same time, and there is no contradiction here. However, I challenge you to read the Luke passage again and see if the natural understanding of it is not indeed chronological. Of course it is, which is why so many translations render the Greek that way.

C – Matthew and Luke disagree about details of Judas' betrayal and demise:

"When Judas, his betrayer, saw that Jesus was condemned, he repented and brought back the thirty pieces of silver to the chief priests and the elders. He said, 'I have sinned by betraying innocent blood.' But they said, 'What is that to us? See to it yourself.' Throwing down the pieces of silver in the temple, he departed, and he went and hanged himself. But the chief priests, taking the pieces of silver, said, 'It is not lawful to put them into the treasury, since they are blood money.' After conferring together, they used them to buy the potter's field as a place to bury foreigners. For this reason that field has been called the Field of Blood to this day." ((Matt. 27:4-8)

"Brothers and sisters, the scripture had to be fulfilled, which the Holy Spirit through David foretold concerning Judas, who became a guide for those who arrested Jesus, for he was numbered among us and was allotted his share in this ministry. (Now this man acquired a field with the reward of his wickedness, and falling headlong, he burst open in the middle, and all his bowels gushed out. This became known to all the residents of Jerusalem, so that the field was called in their language Hakeldama, that is, Field of Blood.)" (Acts 1:16-18)

I know you see the problems here:

In recounting the sad story of Judas' betrayal of Jesus, Matthew says that Judas returned his betrayal payment (30 pieces of silver) to the priests, throwing them down in their presence and showing utter remorse for his act. The priests, however, didn't feel that their returned money should be put into the general Temple fund, because it was "blood money" paid for an act of betrayal resulting in Jesus' death. So they took the money and purchased a plot of land known as "The Potters Field" that would be used to bury "foreigners." And Matthew further tells us this "Potters Field" was also (or alternatively) known as "The Field of Blood" right up to Matthew's own time.

However, Luke (the likely author of Acts) tells us (quoting Peter) that Judas did NOT return the 30 pieces of silver to the Priests, but rather used them to purchase a field (this same "Potters Field?"). And it was in this field that he "fell headlong" and his middle split open, resulting in his bowels gushing out. And it was for THIS reason—-the bloody bowel gushing mess—that this field was called "The Field of Blood."

So, leaving aside the implied contradiction of whether Judas tripped in a field and ended up dead in a bloody mess, or whether he hanged himself in some unknown location, there are two OBVIOUS contradictions here:

1) Matthew says Judas returned the blood money to the priests and *they* purchased a field, while Luke tells us that Judas kept the money and purchased the field *himself*.
2) Matthew says that the reason this Potters Field was called "The Field of Blood" is because it was purchased with "blood money," while Luke tells us the reason is because Judas' midsection exploded in a bloody mess there.

But again, the perfect-Bible warriors have an answer for this:

Judas, by returning the money to the priests, was *ultimately* the one who purchased the Potters Field. "Agency is involved here," they say, and all I can say to that is, "Wut?" Any normal reading of these two passages will result in understanding that one says the priests purchased the field, while the other says Judas did.

And as for the contradictory reasons given for why that field was called "The Field of Blood," I found no answer. That is perhaps because there IS no way to reconcile those two ideas, not even with a convoluted, twisted, forced, jamming of this square peg into the round hole.

D - The four Gospels seem to be utterly confused about the details of what happened on the first Easter:

This problem is a real "whing, dang, doozie" in comparison to some of the others. It has to do with one of the most signature, foundational, and central tenets of the Christian faith—the resurrection of Jesus and the events that surrounded it. Without reproducing all the Gospel accounts here, which would take up at least a couple of pages of this book, I would direct the reader to consult their own Bibles and follow along.

Who are the people involved on that first Easter morning, and what are the events that took place? Let me summarize the problems by quoting from the book *Jesus, Interrupted* (pp. 48-49) by the very able New Testament scholar, Dr. Bart Ehrman:

"Who actually went to the tomb? Was it Mary alone (John 20:1)? Mary and another Mary (Matt. 28:1)? Mary Magdalene, Mary the mother of Kames, and Salome (Mk. 16:1)? Or women who had accompanied Jesus from Galilee to Jerusalem—possibly Mary Magdalene, Joanna, Mary the mother of James, and 'other women' (Luke 24:1; see 23:55)? Had the stone already been rolled away from the tomb (as in Mark 16:4) or was it rolled away by an angel while the women were there (Matthew 28:2)? Whom or what did they see there? An angel (Matthew 28:5)? A young man (Mark 16:5)? Two men (Luke 24:4)? Or nothing and no one (John)? And what were they told? To tell the disciples to 'go to Galilee, where Jesus will meet them (Mark 16:7)? Or to remember what Jesus had told them 'when he was in Galilee,' that he had to die and rise again (Luke 24:7)? Then, do the women tell the disciples what they saw and heard (Matthew 28:8, or do they not tell anyone (Mark 16:8)? If they tell someone, whom do they tell? The eleven disciples (Matthew 28:8)? The eleven disciples and other people (Luke 24:8)? Simon Peter and another unnamed disciple (John 20:2)? What do the disciples do in response? Do they have no response because Jesus himself immediately appears to them (Matthew 20:9)? Do they not believe the women because it seems to be 'an idle tale' (Luke 24:11)? Or do they go to the tomb to see for themselves (John 20:3)?"

Sheesh, trying to "harmonize" all these conflicting details is like trying to fit *a whole bunch* of square pegs into round holes! And if you don't believe that these varying accounts are a huge problem, just sit down with a big note pad, make a few columns with the headings "Who?," "What?," "Where?," and "When?," and see if you can make heads or tails out of it.

Add to this that in the same general time context we have one Gospel writer (Matthew) telling us that Jesus ascended into Heaven from Galilee (in the north of Palestine) and another (Luke) telling us he ascended from Jerusalem (in the south).

At any rate, the Bible purists have long discussed the problems here, and their "answers" to this mass of contradictions range from "we can't expect the Gospel writers to treat historical narrative the same way modern historians do" (Wut?) to a *copy and paste* method of cramming all these non-harmonious details into a single account that looks like a Frankenstein monster. (My apologies to said monster, who at least was a unified "person").

And when you argue that "OK, it's not history in the way we understand history," then how can we read *any* reciting of events in *any* Bible passage and be even moderately assured that that's how it all went down? E.g., did God really create the heavens and the earth in the order alleged? Did Moses really part the Red Sea so that Israel could pass through? Was Jesus really crucified with two other people? And then, Is salvation really afforded only to those who put their faith in Jesus? Is it really true that it's "absent from the body, present with the Lord (2 Cor.)?

Alright, we've seen a few select examples of the massive amount of internal contradictions in the Bible, but what are some of the contradictions the Bible has with modern science?

Chapter Ten

Problems Between the Bible and Science

Perhaps it should be noted at the outset here that there is a difference between "the Bible" and "religion." One might argue that there is no conflict between religion and science, since religion usually refers to a system of faith and worship—i.e., things of a spiritual and non-material nature—and science is concerned with things of a material nature. But there IS a conflict between science and the Bible, because the Bible asserts certain things about the material cosmos which science has definitely disproved.

For example, Genesis chapter 1 describes the creation of the "universe" in this way:

God creates the earth, which is initially formless, empty, and enshrouded by darkness (vv. 1-2). As his spirit (or "a mighty wind") moves over the existing watery chaos, he suddenly creates "light," which is distinguished from the darkness, and the two then follow each other in chronological order, which creates the first "day" (vv. 3-5). Then God creates a "dome" which penetrates the waters and thus establishes those "above" the dome and those "beneath" it, and we have a second "day" (vv. 6-8). Then God gathers the waters beneath the dome (later named "Sky") into one place, naturally exposing some "dry land," and he commands that this dry land produce vegetation suitable for consumption by the not-yet-created humans and animals. So we have the third "day" (vv. 9-13). Then God creates the sun, the moon, and the stars, and hangs them on the underside of the dome for the purposes of establishing not-yet-established Hebrew feasts and a calendar for them, for separating "night" from "day," and for providing light on the earth (vv.14-19)—the fourth "day." Then God created all kinds of marine life, including sea monsters, plus all kinds of birds, and commands them to freely reproduce and fill the skies and the seas. Thus, there is the fifth "day" (vv. 20-23). Next, God creates land animals of all kinds, then "mankind" (Heb. "adam," אדם), and gives mankind authority over all living creatures that are not "human." This "humankind" (male and female) is said to be created "in God's image," *image* being a word in Hebrew ("tselem," צלם) that elsewhere in the Bible means "a physical image." All these creatures, mankind and animals, are to eat the vegetation which God provided for on day three (vv. 24-31). Finally, after six full days of some heavy-duty creating, God rests on the seventh "day" (vv. 2:1-3).

Quite a well-organized, tightly expressed account of how "things came to be," I'd say. But science has something to say about how things came to be, too, and it is in stark opposition to the Genesis account.

For example, there is no physical "dome" covering this planet, as if creation is roughly analogous to something like the Houston Astrodome sports complex in Texas. But that's the picture we get here in Genesis: The earth is ostensibly flat, like a dinner plate, and an inverted "bowl" is placed over it. There are definitely no "waters" above such a non-existent dome; the sun, moon, and stars are not hung on the underside of it; and there are no "windows" (Gen. 7:11; 8:2) placed in this phantom dome that "rain" can come through. We have been aware of this for at least 600 years, when the first truly scientific minds began to seriously observe and describe "heaven and earth." The existence of "day" and "night" are also not independent of one another, because we now understand that Earth is a sphere whose surface faces the sun half the time (day) and is hidden from it half the time (night). In other words, "day" and "night" are always going on *at the same time*, and your position on earth determines which one you are experiencing at any given hour on the clock.

Science has also established that living creatures had a common, simultaneous beginning, and that biological evolution has produced the diversity we see between those creatures. At some time millions of years ago we all got our start in some single-celled bacterium, and since that time, evolution has gone "hog wild" in producing all kinds of living things in various shapes, sizes, and complexity.

There is also a hidden assertion in this Genesis account about the age of the earth and the heavens. You'll notice that Adam (mankind) was said to be created on the sixth day, and we have other parts of the Bible which trace his lineage in genealogies that state the ages of his descendants. So, when you add up all the ages of these people, you get the following time line:

Adam to Noah—about 1056 years.
Noah to Abraham—about 892 years
Abraham to Jesus—about 2000 years
Jesus to now—about 2000 years

If you add all that time up, you come up with about 6000 years for the age of the universe!!! And even if you argue that the genealogies occasionally leave out a generation or two, the most this can suggest is that the earth might be as much as 8000 years old.

But science has firmly established that the universe is MUCH older than that—namely about 13.8 *billion* years old—which is a darn site longer time period than 6000 (or 8000) years. Science has also fixed the age of the earth itself at about 4.5 *billion* years, again a much longer period of time than what Genesis claims. Add to this that we now know that the earth spins on its axis, which is what gives rise to "nights" and "days," that our sun and all the stars in the universe are just gaseous (plasmatic) spheres than burn brightly and are essentially the same in nature, and that the moon itself is not a "light," but a planetary orb that reflects the sun's light, and you see that Genesis dropped the ball here in speaking to our origins. The sun, moon, and stars are not "hung" or "placed" on anything, even though that may appear to be the case from our point of view. Also, rain doesn't happen when "the windows of heaven open" and "the waters above the dome" flow through.

Now those who insist that the Genesis account is true must resort to some extremely convoluted "reasoning" and interpreting to get there. For example, regarding the age of the earth and universe, they claim that God created them with "apparent age." They point to Adam and Eve being created as adults, the animals being created in the same fashion, as well as all vegetation. So when scientists adduce all manner of evidence that the universe is much, much older, they claim that it "only appears that way." They ignore the geologic record, the astronomic record, general physics, biology, and a whole bunch of other established science to do so. They claim that this "firmament" (the inverted bowl) over a flat earth, should rather be translated something like "the expanse" (meaning what you see when you look upwards), and not a firm, material object like the Hebrew word (raqia, רקיע) actually means. After all, this "firmament" supported an ocean above it according to the wording in Genesis 1, and it had "windows" in it. But they'll say, "Oh, that's just 'figurative' language and not meant to be taken literally," evidently not realizing that a "figurative" object (like space or air) could not support tons of water.

There are plenty of other "collisions" between science and the Bible, and here are just a few:

The earth does not "sit upon its foundations" (1 Sam. 2:8; 2 Sam. 22:16; Job 9:16; etc.). But biblical literalists will again say "that's just figurative language."

There are no "ends" to the earth (Isa. 5:26), because it's a sphere. It also does not have "four corners" (Isa. 11:12). But the literalists will holler, "those are *all* just figures of speech."

Stars cannot "fall from the sky" (Isa. 34:4; Mark 13:24-25; etc.), which implies that the earth is stationary and stars are suspended "above" it. The earth is flying through space (at about 67.000 miles per hour around the sun), along with every other orb out there, and if a star—ANY star—ever got even moderately close to this planet, BAD things would happen, not the least of which would be that earth's surface would be fried, and eventually the whole planet would evaporate. Just consider that our "star"—the sun—is about 93 million miles away from earth, and just a short time in the sun by unprotected or fair human skin can cause radiation burns resulting in severe pain. In fact, if I were to lay naked on the beach for as few as 3-4 days, I likely would not survive it. That level of solar radiation exposure can *kill*.

And we know all this from *science*.

In recent years, there has been a proliferation of creationists and pseudo scientists who, motivated by religious faith, have produced a fair number of articles, blogs, vlogs, podcasts, websites, books, and other media intended to undergird and support a literal interpretation of the Bible. Most of the people involved are not actual scientists, but a few are. Which only goes to prove that intelligence is not a guarantor of rational thought and acceptance of empirical evidence. Some of the smartest people are the most deluded (e.g., The Unabomber, Elon Musk, Elizabeth Holmes, etc. etc.). But it doesn't take a rocket scientist to observe that diseases don't come from demons (Mk. 9:17-27; Lk. 13:11; etc.), dead folks don't come alive again (at least after a few minutes or more), no star can ever "fall to earth (Rev. 6:13), and waving a striped branch in front of cattle can't cause those cattle to become striped themselves (Gen. 30:37-43).

So science and religion (a belief system claiming to identify things neither seen nor heard) may not inherently conflict with one another, but science and the Bible most definitely do. However, to the extent that one's religion depends upon a literal interpretation of the Bible, one can say that science and religion *do* conflict.

So how has the Bible affected mankind, both collectively and individually? That's next.

Chapter Eleven
The Bible's Influence on Individual Believers

Chapter 3 discussed, in very summary fashion, the influence of the Bible on history. Here I want to discuss its very direct influence, both good and ill, on the individuals who read and believe it.

Life is a tough gig. It is tougher on some than others, depending on one's socioeconomic status and on the actual events that occur during their lifetimes. Those with more abundant means generally suffer less than the poor, and those with extravagant wealth suffer less than all other classes of people. (At least in terms of basic survival needs). The child born in rank poverty in the Sudan suffers such horrific ills as hunger, sickness, and the constant threat of death. The child born in New York's Upper East Side most generally never has to worry about food insufficiency or basic good nutrition, lack of medical care, clothing, and instability of social order.

But most human beings are vulnerable to the ugly sides of life, namely serious disappointments, emotional pain, anxieties of various sorts, death of loved ones and friends, various acts of violence, loneliness, and so on. And these can be gut-wrenching at times, regardless of your economic status. My own experience was that of being born into the middle class, then economic insecurity after my father's early death at 47 years old, then being a mostly broke college student for many years, then being a club musician with oscillating financial status, then finally being upper middle class as a result of starting my own business and being successful.

But during all that time I suffered disappointments in terms of job opportunities, romantic relationships, familial squabbles, occasional illnesses, roller coaster economic health, and general anxiety about the pressures of life. Add to that certain religious anxieties I had about what was true/an afterlife/my true purpose, etc. and I'd say life was only occasionally happy for me. And when it was unhappy, it often was VERY unhappy.

So I get it. Life is, at times, painful and depressing for most people. And the Bible has provided comfort to millions over the centuries as a "solution" to their questions and problems. For example, when someone that we love dies, the Bible is cited as proof that the person is in Heaven, just waiting for us when *we* die. (It serves to mitigate the pain of the loss if you believe that you will, indeed, see these people again in a utopian existence). The Bible also provides hope for dealing with seemingly random hits we take, like the loss of a job/a lover/a friend, an unexpected massive bill, a sickness or disability, etc. "If you pray," it says, "God will answer you and remedy that problem" (in one way or the other). If you are raised in a faith tradition that says you're inherently a "sinner," then the Bible says you will be forgiven if you repent of the sin and ask for forgiveness. If you have, as I did in my late teens and early twenties, fundamental questions about life and your purpose in it, then the Bible says you're God's personal creation, he has a plan for your life, and you can rest easy that you therefore have value and that God will guide you to fulfill that purpose.

And whether those claims are true or not, many have believed them and enjoyed great comfort when life rains on them.

But it has also spurred quite a bit of negativity and hate as well as peace and comfort. It has been used to spread the notion of "original sin," the idea that Adam and Eve were initially pure, but after their disobedience in the Garden of Eden, they became sinful by nature, and that this sin nature has been passed on to every one of their descendants (i.e., every human being, including you and me). Therefore, everyone is inherently a sinner and needs God's salvation. (Various religious institutions who rely on the Bible for their dogma disagree on *how* that salvation is be accomplished, but they all agree that it is necessary for everyone). This inflicts a sense of guiltiness on those who believe that, and can often affect one's self-image and sense of self-worth. In both the Hebrew Bible (Old Testament) and the New Testament, certain "sins" are specifically enumerated: drunkenness, lying, murder, adultery, fornication, testifying falsely against another, failure to impregnate your widowed sister-in-law so as to continue your brother's lineage, failure to believe in Israel's god or his alleged son Jesus, pursuit of any other god than the Hebrew/Christian one, failure to offer the correct sacrifice (in Israelite times), cursing or disobeying your parents, engaging in "sorcery," failure to support the poor, engaging in homosexuality, divorcing your wife except in cases where she was adulterous, general hatred, coveting something that someone else has, arrogance or pride, gossiping, jealousy, vengeance, and etc.

Another way in which it contributes negatively to humankind is in its allegations about "Hell." The Bible is not exactly clear about the *location* or *nature* of this place, but it's no picnic to be sure (sometimes it's eternal fire, accompanied by weeping and gnashing of teeth, sometimes it's outer darkness, sometimes it's flames but you can see across the divide between it and Abraham's bosom). Hell is not mentioned at all in the Hebrew Bible (Old Testament), and in fact most of the references to afterlife in that collection of books concern a place called "Sheol" (Heb. Sheol, שׁאול). Sheol, according to the Judaism reflected in the Hebrew Bible, is a shadowy, spirit-like place where the "shades" (people who died on earth) meander about in a wispy half-existence. They do not remember their past life on earth, and are merely shadowy, half-existent beings, cut off from God. It is not a pleasant place, but it is not a place of torture (like Hell is described in the New Testament).

Yet another way it is negatively influential is that it is often used by right-wing political movements (especially in the United States) to support their ill-bred notions of "God's will." For example, the Bible is often quoted as condemning homosexuality (and it does in a couple of places) and is thus used to divest non-cisgender people of their civil rights (marriage, jobs, participation in sports, etc.). It was used during the Civil War era to justify the practice of slavery. It is used by some Christian Dominionist groups to support their (non-biblical) view that our country's laws should be shaped by "Christian" morality. (The Constitution *clearly* forbids this, however). It is used by some to suggest that Jews are "God's chosen people," and Arabs are descendants of the less-favored-by-God wife of Abraham, Hagar. In this trope, some Christians see *carte blanche* for anything Israel wants to do in Palestine. (E.g., increase settlements and move Palestinians out of their homes and land). The recent slaughter of 35,000 innocents (at this counting) in Gaza is justified by saying, "God gave Palestine to Israel, so it is their right to do most anything to complete their occupation of it."

I have personally seen it used to bust up relationships, for example when the "do not be unequally yoked with unbelievers" verse (2 Cor. 6:14) is cited as reason for discontinuing a platonic or non-platonic union. I've seen it used (hundreds of times) to pass judgement on someone else's character or on their value as a human being. I've observed instances of it being used by a mother to drown her children "to save them from this evil world" (Andrea Yates from Texas), or by a (deluded) "righteous warrior" to bomb abortion clinics or murder abortion doctors (like Eric Robert Rudolph and others). I've seen it used by unscrupulous TV pastors to bilk the naïve out of their money, promising "more money will come to you if just give us *yours*." And history is replete with the number of times so-called "end-time prophets" have declared that "Jesus is coming to initiate the Apocalypse on *this* date or *that* date," and deluded followers liquidate all their assets and give the money to these "prophets" or to some other cause. (Only to be left penniless, "holding the bag" as it were, the day after this 2nd Coming did not take place). And the use of the Book of Revelation—with its ancient symbolic and apocalyptic language—is used exponentially to tie modern realities to its symbolic language. (E.g., "the mark of the beast" in Rev.13:18 to refer to modern ways of retail commerce like credit cards or proposed chips to be implanted under the skin of a person, the "seven hills" of Revelation to identify "Rome" and the current Catholic Church (as "evil" things), the "ten toes" of Daniel's dream image (Dan. 2:42-44) as a reference to the European Common Market of just a few years ago. And so forth.

But there is one overall malign influence the Bible has in a macro sense. It claims, over and over within its pages, to reveal truths for which there is *no* empirical evidence. As mentioned before, no one has seen God (Yahweh or any other), no one has seen a Devil or a demon, no one has seen Heaven, no one has seen Hell, no one has seen an angel, no one has seen an actual miracle (in the sense of an event where natural law or the laws of physics are suspended), no one has seen a dead person come back to life (in the true sense), and so forth. Oh, there are plenty of people throughout history who have claimed to have seen these things, but not one of them has produced any empirical evidence to support those claims. And one wonders—with the introduction of both audio and video equipment over the last 80 years or so—why that is so. Why it is so, I suggest, is because those kinds of supernatural events are not happening.

And here is the point: *The Bible, as it is read by everyday folk, conditions a person's mind to accept the unseeable and unhearable as* **realities**. In other words, a Bible-believing person is much more likely to believe in things that aren't actually happening than someone who is not a Bible-believer. This is why recent sociological studies have shown that conspiracy theories are believed by evangelical Christians much more than by non-believers. And, in America, conspiracy theories and "fake news" are rampant (mostly on the right).

The cure for this, of course, is to educate people in the skill of critical thinking. Christopher Hitchens used to say, "Extraordinary claims require extraordinary evidence," and he was right. As mankind moves into the future, it will do itself a huge favor if it can relinquish the "belief without evidence" model, and accept only what can reasonably be proved. And there is no better time in a person's life than when they are young to start being taught this way of thinking. I'm looking at you, educators, to accomplish this task.

So the Bible is a much-used source to accomplish all sorts of evil and good, whether it is being interpreted correctly (the original meaning and intent of its authors/compilers/editors) or not.

And now is a good time to consider just *what*, exactly, the Bible is.

Chapter Twelve

What is the Bible, Really?

It is helpful, at this point, to very briefly summarize some of the previous information in this book as we look to determine, once and for all, just what the Bible is.

No book—or collection of books in this case—is born outside of the culture and time period of its origin. Shakespeare's plays were a product of his own age and culture (and you better understand some of those things if you wish to correctly understand his works), Solzhenitsyn's "The Gulag Archipelago" requires some understanding of Russian politics and the culture of his time, George R. R. Martin's "A Song of Ice and Fire" (re-named "The Game of Thrones" for the TV production) requires at least a modicum of understanding of medieval culture and language idiom, and so forth. Every piece of literature ever written is birthed in a particular time period of history and in the cultural norms of the author's life. And so it is with the Bible.

The Bible did not suddenly float down from Heaven, neatly printed out with verse and chapter divisions, bound by a leather cover, translated into one language, with titles for each included book. As you'll recall, the earliest books of the Bible were generated by the religious elite within the various Judaisms that were being practiced inside ancient Israel, and as the centuries passed more books were written (or the oral traditions were collected and edited) to instruct and edify the Jews within the nation. This process, from beginning to end, perhaps started as early as the 800s BCE (BC), and came to a close in or around the 200s BCE (BC).

When the offshoot of Judaism, which we now call "Christianity," began to take root, the books of the New Testament were soon written, perhaps beginning around 50 CE (AD) and continuing to around 125 CE (AD). Other books were written in both the tradition of Judaism which did not make the cut into the Hebrew Bible (Old Testament) canon, and many books were written in the post-Jesus period which did not make it into the now-accepted canons of the New Testament (Catholic, Protestant, Eastern Orthodox). "The Book of Jashar" (Josh. 10:12-13; 2 Sam. 1:17-27), for instance, is not found in any Hebrew Bible (cause it did not survive), and "The Gospel of Thomas" is not found in any New Testament.

So the question is, "Is this collection of books, 'the Bible,' a message that was dictated, or inspired, or composed *in any way* by God, or is it merely the product of different individuals and groups within ancient Hebrew culture, composed over many centuries?"

Perhaps we should consider varying answers to this question. Those who claim that the Bible is the "Word of God," accurate in all that it says about matters both earthly and divine, are well represented by this formal statement of The Chicago Council on Inerrancy (1978):

Being wholly and verbally God-given, Scripture is without error or fault in all its teaching, no less in what it states about God's acts in creation, about the events of world history, and about its own literary origins under God, than in its witness to God's saving grace in individual lives. (Point #4 in the initial summary.)

So what this statement (which is followed by most evangelical Christians) says about the Bible is that God gave its verbal contents to the authors, and that those contents are 100% accurate regarding either spiritual or historical matters. In other words, if the Bible speaks on the origin of the universe and all of its life forms, or on Israel's or the early Christians' history, it is completely and wholly word-for-word accurate. No error whatsoever exists anywhere in its pages. For them, science is wrong about biological evolution, diseases being caused by breakdowns in the functional physical order of things rather than by demons, the age of the universe, the nature of mankind, etc. *The Bible is 100% correct about anything it says, period.* (I often heard this from the pastor of the evangelical church I attended in my early faith days: "The Bible says, I believe it, that settles it!").

This view is a little different than what the Catholics say about the matter. In the theological pronouncements of The Second Vatican Council (1962-65), it included this statement on the nature of the Bible:

The Scriptures, together with Tradition are the supreme rule of faith (DV, n. 21). They flow out of the same divine wellspring and together make up one sacred deposit of faith from which the Church derives her certainty about revelation. The Scriptures are a product of, and witness to, the living tradition in its early stages; and the living tradition of the Church faithfully passes on the word of God.

If you didn't catch the meaning, it could be restated this way: The Bible is the Word of God, but along with the Apostolic Tradition (the succession of Popes and the living tradition passed on from the time of Jesus until the present), the two form the true word of God. In other words, the Bible is to be regarded as authoritative and divine in origin, but only as it is interpreted by the Holy Catholic Church. No single Catholic believer may read the Bible and form his or her own opinion about what the words mean, as this is the Church's domain. (In truth, this is sort of equivalent, in practice, to how Protestant believers treat their Bibles. They read them and form their own interpretations, to be sure, but they rely on their pastors or Bible study teachers to guide them in their opinions on many biblical issues).

Jewish folk have even a little wider degree of latitude in forming their impressions of Scripture. There is a long and voluminous history of

Jewish commentators on the Hebrew Bible, and these consist mostly of the musings of hundreds of rabbis collected in the "Talmud" (meaning "learning," or "teaching"). The Talmud contains both The Mishnah ("learning by repetition") and the Gemarah ("the completion"). There are also further "Midrash" (rabbinic "interpretations") that have been collected over the years, leaving our Jewish brethren with lots of options for biblical interpretation. And unlike the Protestant and Catholic stances on the Bible, there really are no overall, authoritative, uniform statements coming from either the more orthodox (conservative) or reformed (liberal) communities in modern Judaism.

It is worth mentioning here another Protestant form of Christianity and its view of the Bible. It's known as "neo-orthodoxy," and it originated as a critical response to the liberal Protestantism which was common in the 18th Century CE (AD) and just before World War 1. Its most famous proponent was Karl Barth, but the names of Paul Tillich and Emil Brunner should be thrown into the mix as premier thinkers. The position of the neo-orthodox, in general, was that the Bible is indeed a mere human product, and thus not to be believed in matters of history or absolute divine truth, but that by reading it, it can *"become the word of God" as the reader communes with God.* This philosophy informs a boatload of modern liberal Christian denominations (Methodism, liberal Presbyterianism, liberal Lutheranism, etc.). But its fundamental assertion that a "new" kind of conservative orthodoxy should replace the more materialist and humanist liberal Christianity is followed by a huge amount of modern biblical scholars and clerics.

However, what is common to all of these views is the following assertion: In some sense, the Bible, whether accurate in its particulars or not, pulls back the curtain and reveals truths that cannot be visually seen or audibly heard by mankind. Nobody has ever seen "god," an "angel," a "demon," "Satan," "heaven," "hell," or anything that may be referred to as "supernatural." (Nobody that is credible, anyway, in my view). Many persons have claimed to have seen some of these beings or places, but upon close examination these persons cannot be deemed to have actually done so. Many modern pastors or Bible teachers claim to have "conversed with God" in a two-way conversation, but none have produced any actual evidence of that. Many have claimed to engage in supernatural healing of others, but lots of documentaries and journalistic evaluations have proved that such things have never happened. Once, in my younger and wilder years, I thought I saw some bizarre-looking creatures on the wall of my bedroom while I was tripping on acid, but upon further sober reflection, I realized that I had not.

But what is key here is that the Bible *actively asserts* supernatural realities on nearly every page. It claims to answer questions over which mankind has puzzled for millennia. It claims there is "another reality" not observable by the human eye or ear, or by the astronomer's telescope. So we are left with evaluating *whether or not these assertions are true.*

So given the fact that the Bible's books are massively inconsistent in their own descriptive or historical claims, and that the whole thing is in severe conflict with the "big" truths revealed by science, what should our evaluation of these claims be?

And here is the answer, and the whole point of this book:

The Bible is not, in any sense, a revelation of things beyond the veil of the material and observable world. It tells us nothing about the potential existence of a god, about what any potential deity may require of us, about what may happen when we die, or about anything supernatural at all. It is a collection of books, spurred by the specific life events of the early Hebrews (and later by the early Christians who were evolving out of existing Judaisms), and that's about it. It is a tremendously interesting book, and of great value as a peek inside the minds and struggles of these early peoples, but it is no "communication" from the god Yahweh (or any other god).

And what "singes my shorts" (or "rattles my rumpus room") about it all is that very intelligent people—biblical scholars who populate theological seminaries and universities across the world, and who can run circles around me in terms of their encyclopedic knowledge of biblical and related studies, plus intelligent people in general—still cling to this Bible as if either Judaism or Christianity is nevertheless true. Many of them KNOW better (or *should* know better), because in their vast acquisition of information about how cultures evolve and produce religious ideas which are often written down into books, it is apparent that the Bible is just another book in a long line of literature produced by these cultures to soothe the very real angst that we all have experienced about "what the Hell is going on here in this thing we experience as 'life.'"

I mean, I sort of get it. Many of these folks, like me in my earlier progressive journey out of Christianity, don't want to "throw the baby out with the bath water." (I.e., completely abandon their religious beliefs, even though retaining them creates a cognitive dissonance within them). Plus, life is still hard, and for some folks it's just too much to let go of that thing that has helped them cope with its difficulties and challenges. Believe me, *I get it*. It was not easy for me, by any means, to abandon Christianity. But one thing that I have always been able to do, no matter how hard it was, is to follow my logical mind in the pursuit of truth. I cannot, even if I wanted to, accept as true what I know to be false. For example, at certain times I wanted to believe that someone I had been dating was still in love with me, but the facts (her behavior, speech, and disposition) told me the opposite. It was tough, but I accepted it. And such was the case when I finally realized that the Bible, and all of the related religious dogma I had learned and submitted myself to, was NOT what I thought it was. It was just a book, spawning popular religious "lessons," but un-credible on any level, and revealing *nothing* about things seen or unseen.

I finally landed, philosophically, square in the camp of classic *agnosticism*. More specifically, I concede that I have no idea, whatsoever, if a divine being exists, or if our human consciousness continues after death. I've seen no evidence of either, but I don't deny the possibility of their existence. But what I reject, affirmatively, is that the Bible (or any other book, religion, or philosophy) is a credible witness to such things. Said another way, I know quite a bit more about what is *not* true, than what *may* be true. To be sure, if any deity were to appear to me, or in the sky, or through my computer, or on the ceiling above my bed, etc.—and start talking—I would grab a notebook and start madly taking notes. I'd whip out the recorder on my cell phone, activate my Go Pro camera, turn off the TV, and just listen and show utter obeisance to said deity. And after that, I'd probably start calling everyone I know to relate that appearance, and jump onto social media to jabber about it incessantly. But so far, no such event has occurred. (And I've been around for a while).

And as far as how I form my own personal morality, I follow two basic principles: 1) Do good, and 2) Do no harm. These two very simple precepts often require deeper thought in order to know—with regard to specific and sometimes complicated situations—what is "good" and what "causes no harm." But the fundamental ideas in these two principles is always what drives my search for answers.

The subtitle of this book is "and why the answer really matters." That is, whatever the Bible actually is—whether a direct communication from God, or just literature produced by the ancient Hebrews and Christians—is the question of the ages.

If it actually is God's communication to us earthlings, then I can't imagine any other book that has more significance. *The eternal, unseen, God telling us "what's what" in life!!!* Wow! If this were true, then I believe that NOTHING ELSE in the sphere of human existence even comes close to its importance.

Human society is constantly musing about possible life on other planets, claiming that aliens have indeed appeared at various places and times right here on our planet. They speculate that these more advanced beings might have answers that we don't have regarding the universe, and that they could answer scientific and medical questions we haven't yet resolved. We dig in the dirt (archaeology), as if we might find answers to questions that the ancients uniquely possessed. We launch highly sophisticated telescopes and science experiments into space (Hubble, Webb, etc.), hoping to solve riddles long posed by the progressive revelation about the universe that science has initiated.

Yet, if the Bible is a "letter from God," it must be regarded as THE ultimate answer to all of our fundamental questions. And it's funny, most of those who claim that it is (the Word of God) have read precious little of it. It's sort of like, "God sent me a letter, but I haven't read all of it." "Wut?" If a romantic interest of yours sent you an email, or even a snail mail, would you only read a few sections of it here and there? Most of us wouldn't — we'd read the whole thing, start to finish. But those who shout loudest about it being "the Word of God" have, in a majority of cases, never read "the whole thing." (By the way, this is somewhat understandable, because the entire Bible is the size of about 7 or 8 good-sized books, it references cultural traditions completely foreign to modern society, and in places it's hard to follow. And yet, if it's God's communication to us, wouldn't it be important to read the whole thing anyway?).

However, the summary of evidence related earlier in this book has—I hope—convinced you that the Bible is nothing more than a collection of books generated by peoples who shared our own inquisitiveness about life and all of its travails.

And given its internal contradictions, and its contradictions with certain realties (facts) that science has now established about the universe, it is patently irrational to claim that any god has authored it. I mean, I suppose you could still say that, but then you'd have to concede that this god can't keep his story straight, didn't know about the origin of the universe and earthly man, and thereby is peddling falsehoods. And if one part (or many parts) of the Bible is demonstrably untrue, can you really believe *anything* it says? Of course not. Imagine if your spouse or lover told you that they were going to spend the weekend with a girlfriend across town, but you later accidentally found out they traveled out of state to spend two days in a motel with a boyfriend (this actually happened to me). I ask you, can you ever really 100% trust what they tell you in the future? I think not.

So, if the Bible is not what so many claim or hope that it is, what do we do with it? I have some ideas.

Chapter Thirteen

What Should We Do with the Bible?

The possibility that the Bible will cease to be an influence in modern human culture is highly doubtful—at least not within my lifetime, or the lifetimes of some generations to come. And the false tropes that it has given rise to—the existence of the god Yahweh, the notions of sin/the devil/demons/Hell/Heaven/effective prayer/divine judgement/Armageddon/the Rapture/true miracles/etc.—are likely to endure in the belief systems of humanity for quite a while.

So, the first order of business, I think, is to get rid of all those notions and retire them to dust bin of other ancient myths. This is not to say that one should become *amoral* (without a set of moral principles), but only that the Bible's alleged moralities and realities should be abandoned as having no authority from any god or any basis in fact.

For example, there is no such thing as *sin* as the Bible defines it. (It claims that God put out a list of *no-no's*, and if you do one of those *no-no's*, it's "a sin"). There are acts that human beings do (murder, rape, lying, violence, injustice, selfishness, etc.) that should definitely be considered morally bad or repugnant. But that's different than saying that by doing those things you have offended a god and thus committed a *sin*.

As another example, let's once and for all dispense with this nonsense of "Hell." The Bible itself is not clear on the subject, but since we know the Bible is just the baseless speculations of ancient peoples living in the Near East during the Bronze and Iron Ages, let's eradicate this barbaric concept from our global consciousness once and for all. You're not going there, I'm not going there, nobody is going there. *It doesn't exist.*

And so on and so forth for ALL the Bible's themes of Heaven, demons, Satan, Armageddon, etc.

And it doesn't matter if you're a conservative evangelical Christian, a Jew, a Catholic or Orthodox Christian, a "liberal" Christian, a Bible academic, etc.—let's begin to reject using the Bible as a credible source that illuminates *any* alleged reality happening beyond the veil of our material world. It isn't that. And we should become purists that 100% reject using it for that purpose.

So what should we do with this book that has influenced global culture for over 2000 years?

I have a couple of suggestions, and maybe you have others:

1) Let's treat it for what it is—a massive collection of different (and often contradictory) ideas circulating in the area of Palestine between about 1000 BCE (BC) and about 125 CE (AD). As previously mentioned, it gives us a direct peek into the collective mind of the Hebrews and Christians living in that time and in that geography, and for that alone it has academic and historical value.

Similarly, if I want to understand something of ancient Greek culture in the 7th Cent. BCE (BC), I can read Homer's *The Iliad* and *The Odyssey*. If I want to understand something of the cultural rumblings happening within America in the middle of the 19th Cent. CE (AD), I can read Harriet Beecher Stowe's *Uncle Tom's Cabin*; or, for early 20th Cent. CE (AD) American cultural and economic issues, I can read John Steinbeck's *The Grapes of Wrath*. If I'm curious about medieval English culture in the 16th and 17th Cents. CE (AD), then I can read any of Shakespeare's plays. And so it is with the Bible—culturally illuminating, yes, but revelatory of alleged supernatural realties, NO!

2) If we don't wish to "throw the baby out with the bath water" (ignore it entirely), and are just not able to culturally or emotionally "kick it to the curb," then let's focus only on some of its more positive contents. For example:

You shall not take vengeance or bear a grudge against any of your people, but you shall love your neighbor as yourself.... (Lev. 19:18).

In everything do to others as you would have them do to you.... (Matt. 7:12)

Love is patient; love is kind; love is not envious or boastful or arrogant or rude. It does not insist on its own way; it is not irritable; it keeps no record of wrongs; it does not rejoice in wrongdoing but rejoices in the truth. It bears all things, believes all things, hopes all things, endures all things. Love never ends.... (1 Cor. 13:4-8)

Do not forsake wisdom, and she will protect you; love her, and she will watch over you. The beginning of wisdom is this: Get wisdom. Though it cost all you have, get understanding. (Prov. 4:6-7).

Who is wise and understanding among you? Show by your good life that your works are done with gentleness born of wisdom. But if you have bitter envy and selfish ambition in your hearts, do not be boastful and false to the truth. (James 3:13)

Pride goes before destruction and a haughty spirit before a fall. (Prov. 16:18)

Pretty good stuff, eh? Of course it is. Exhortations about the primacy of love and treating others as you'd like to be treated, loving your neighbor *and* yourself, developing wisdom as a requisite life skill, avoiding retaliation against those who have wronged you, guarding against a haughty spirit, etc. are all pretty good pieces of advice in any culture or time period, I'd say.

So the Bible has some good things in it, as do many pieces or collections of literature. But it has nothing in it that pulls back the veil on supernatural "realities" (if there even are such things). And if there is no other message you take from the journey here in this book, please heed this one: It is imperative that we stop treating it—*in any way, shape, or form*—as a word from beyond that reveals things we can't see or hear.

One of my favorite American politicians from the past is Thomas Jefferson. This American Founding Father had an approach to the Bible that I largely agree with. As a child of The Enlightenment, he rejected portions of the Bible that spoke of miraculous events (events that run counter to the laws of physics and natural law). But he greatly admired the moral teachings of Jesus, and in his later life he constructed a New Testament for his own use. He took a razor blade to all the New Testament passages which described Jesus doing supernatural, miraculous things (like turning water into wine, healing people, resurrecting after his death, and so forth). This left only the "moral" teachings of Jesus, and those were what he sought to model in his life. This book survives today under the title *The Life and Morals of Jesus of Nazareth*.

So it is my hope for humanity as a whole that they become more and more focused on the "here and now" as opposed to the "there and later," so that we can continually improve the quality of our collective existence here on this planet. This requires that we throw off all the dogmas, moral musings, edicts, and the innate "othering" of those who don't look, speak, believe, or behave as we do in our little corners of the world. And I don't mean just those who follow the Judaisms/Christianities fostered by the Bible, but also those who follow *all* religions which are fostered by "holy books" or religious traditions. Life is, or can be, a pretty wonderful thing when we all commit to "treating our neighbors as ourselves," and when we work towards a common goal of together solving the very real and deep-seated problems that universally permeate life—in the present time, and with no view towards the alleged divinities conjured in these books and who are allegedly "telling us what to do." No, it's *on us*, and if we are to have a better, more peaceful and prosperous world, it's only we who can accomplish it.

All that said, I have a few final thoughts.

Chapter Fourteen
Final Thoughts

Once you liberate yourself from considering the Bible and its precepts authoritative for your life, you are free to form your own morals and values. After all, the morals and precepts you find in its pages are themselves ones conjured up by other human beings. And as you do, I recommend that you use *empathy* as a basis for forming those values. Have you been cheated or lied to by others? If so, you know that it doesn't feel good, so endeavor not to do that to your fellow human beings. Have you been physically struck by others? It doesn't feel good, right? So don't strike others. Have you had relationships in which the other person was excessively selfish? That is hurtful, as well, so don't mimic their behavior. And so forth.

Empathy is something that is available to every person if they are willing to utilize it, and that empathy is a natural function of being a living, conscious human being. Some folks seem never to have marshalled it within themselves, and their lives are just one continuous display of "what's in it for ME?" It's *me, me, me* at every turn. Of course, you have to be self-interested on some level, such as providing food, medicine, and shelter for yourself, and learning how to develop and care for your own mental health, but having your *own* interest as primary with *every* interaction is no way to live. I have known a few people who seem never to have done something for the benefit of another without demanding something in return. Is that really a legacy that anyone wants to leave in their wake? We only get "one go around in life" as far as we know for sure, and a life spent stepping on others in order to accumulate as much as is humanly possible for oneself seems like a poor way to live it. After all, you're "not gonna take it with you."

On the flip side, liberating yourself from the Bible's malevolent influence can have very positive effects on your happiness and contentment in life. If you're constantly anxious about some god watching your every move, or some current or delayed punishment for bad things you may have done, you will likely experience a great deal of unhappiness—unhappiness in the form of guilt, fear, self-sabotage, and puppet-like behavior (doing kind things merely because a god told you to do them). And that's no way to live, either.

There is the additional issue of how the Bible and its dependent religions provide a coping mechanism for all of life's troubles. And I get it. When we experience the death of a loved one, it is a great comfort to believe that we will see that person again "in Heaven." It somewhat softens the blow and the trauma of this very ugly reality, and somehow makes the loss at least bearable. (Again, as an agnostic, I have no idea at all if there is a conscious afterlife. I just know it won't be the one described in any part of the Bible).

And there is the emotional stability it can provide when you believe that most of life's questions have been answered in the Bible. I've seen drug addicts and drunks jettison their dependence on these substances when they "get converted" and substitute their new-found beliefs as their primary coping mechanism for life. And one might say that this is good, since leaving harmful substances behind and instead interacting with a new belief system is certainly more physically healthy. But in reality it is also just replacing one deceptive influence with another deceptive one.

Yes, life is a tough gig, and there all kinds of coping mechanisms used by people to deal with its dark side. Besides biologic substances and religion, people use work, sex, food, cults, gaming, doom scrolling, sports, and a host of other distractions to escape unpleasant or hurtful realities. And it's totally understandable. But it's not wise, as distraction is not a good substitute for facing down life's troubles and finding a way to cope with it *au naturelle*. Because no matter how much you distract yourself from your troubles, they are still there when you come off a booze or drug bender, or from being in the general non-real world of any kind of distractive behavior.

And let me be real clear here. I am *not* saying that there is anything inherently harmful about occasional and recreational "partying" with alcohol or drugs, or with immersing yourself into your job (within reason), or with playing video games or scrolling social media sites on the internet, or frequent (consensual) sex, etc.—*as long as you aren't wholly dependent of any of them for your happiness or sanity*. Sometimes spending a weekend at the beach with a cooler of beer, or visiting a bar with a live band playing, or sparking a blunt, or binge-watching an interesting Netflix-produced series on the telly, or reading a trashy romance novel is "just what the doctor ordered" for "recharging your batteries" or getting your mind off unpleasant things. But again, if any of these activities are constant or indispensable necessities for plowing through life, then I'd suggest you step back and evaluate the larger situation.

And let me also be clear that I am *not* saying that people with chronic anxiety disorders shouldn't take anti-anxiety medications prescribed by their doctors (as long as the doctor is genuinely trying to help them in a larger, comprehensive program of reducing their underlying anxieties). Of course these kinds of substances (and others) are helpful in managing one's mental health.

But Bible-based (and other book-based) religions are inherently fantasy, and in the end they cause more problems than they solve. You are, merely by virtue of being born of a woman, inherently and incomprehensively *valuable*—and it's not because some god says so or because of your supposed place in some "divine drama." Regardless of your gender, your ethnicity, your economic or professional status in life, or your address, you are the crowning achievement of all of "creation." As Joni Mitchell once remarked (in song), "We are stardust, we are GOLDEN." And she was right.

You don't need a Bible or holy book to tell you that—it's just a fact.

And it's my sincere hope that we can, as humankind, divest ourselves of all religious dogma and philosophy, all holy books, and just get on with the business of improving life for each other, one and all.

And let my last word here be that, although I will not have met most of you who will read these words, I sincerely wish every one of you a happy and contented life. A life without the shackles of religious dogma and prejudice, and a life that can be quite beautiful and satisfying without those things. To the extent I can, I love you all, and if there is another plane of existence after this one in which we meet, I greatly look forward to it.

But for this life, I hope that we—as collective humanity—eventually become enlightened enough to live it without Bibles, religions, or other authoritarian philosophies that only dull the beauty of this one.

John Lennon apparently felt the same way:

Imagine there's no heaven
It's easy if you try
No hell below us
Above us, only sky
Imagine all the people
Livin' for today…

Imagine there's no countries
It isn't hard to do
Nothing to kill or die for
And no religion, too
Imagine all the people
Livin' life in peace…

You may say I'm a dreamer
But I'm not the only one
I hope someday you'll join us
And the world will be as one.

Imagine no possessions
I wonder if you can
No need for greed or hunger
A brotherhood of man
Imagine all the people
Sharing all the world...

You may say I'm a dreamer
But I'm not the only one
I hope someday you'll join us
And the world will live as one.

(From the song, "Imagine;" 1971)

www.ingramcontent.com/pod-product-compliance
Lightning Source LLC
Chambersburg PA
CBHW050444010526
44118CB00013B/1668